SKINNY SANDWICHES

DESIRÉE WITKOWSKI, D.T.R.

Surrey Books

CHICAGO

SKINNY SANDWICHES is published by Surrey Books, Inc.
230 E. Ohio St., Suite 120, Chicago, IL 60611.

First edition: 1 2 3 4 5

This book is manufactured in the United States of America.

Library of Congress Cataloging-in-Publication data:

Witkowski, Desirée.
    Skinny sandwiches / by Desirée Witkowski.
    175p. cm.
    Includes index.
    ISBN 0-940625-56-3 (pbk. : alk. paper)
    1. Sandwiches. 2. Low-cholesterol diet—Recipes. 3. Low-calorie
diet—Recipes. I. Title.
TX818.W58 1995
641.8'4—dc20   95-13530
                                       CIP

Editorial and production: *Bookcrafters, Inc., Chicago*
Art Director: *Hughes & Co., Chicago*
Cover and interior illustrations by *Laurel DiGangi*
Back cover photos courtesy *California Olive Industry*

For free catalog and prices on quantity purchases, contact Surrey Books at the
address above.

This title is distributed to the trade by Publishers Group West.

Other titles in the "Skinny" Cookbooks Series:

Skinny Beef
Skinny Chicken
Skinny Chocolate
Skinny Cookies, Cakes & Sweets
Skinny Grilling
Skinny One-Pot Meals
Skinny Pasta

Skinny Pizzas
Skinny Potatoes
Skinny Sauces & Marinades
Skinny Seafood
Skinny Soups
Skinny Spices
Skinny Vegetarian Entrées

This book is dedicated, in loving memory,
to my dear friend Clancy Roff, the father
I never had.

CONTENTS

INTRODUCTION

T hroughout their history, sandwiches have been both socially
scorned and exalted. Reduced to the lowly status of "fast-food,"
sandwiches have been, at best, simple plebeian affairs. Recently, with a
renewed interest in gourmet foods combined with health concerns, sandwiches are back in vogue as a desirable vehicle for weight loss. Never
before has the sandwich been more popular, healthier, or embraced so
many gastronomical possibilities. May this book help you discover the
healthy sandwich!

There is something satisfying about a sandwich: the down-to-earth
texture of wholesome bread encasing a delicious filling. A well-made sandwich consists of foods necessary for a *nutritionally complete* meal or
snack. Aesthetically pleasing, sandwiches can be skinny, which means low
in fat, high in protein, fiber, and B vitamins. A skinny sandwich also carries

the comforting lift of eating something you love that won't go to your hips. Yes, a skinny sandwich is a comfort food.

Sandwiches Can Make Dieting Fun

"Dieting" to most people is synonymous with following a prescribed menu or eating a limited number of foods. Sandwich variety, on the other hand, is unlimited, and you can eat the foods you love.

Most dieters' weakness is simply eating too much, or "portion control." Controlling the amount of food eaten is addressed by many weight-control clinics by centering their program around prepackaged, expensive, low-calorie meals they sell to their clients. You can do this yourself with sandwiches—and it happens naturally because sandwiches are high in complex carbohydrates and protein, which means they're filling as well as an automatic single serving.

At least once a day invest in a sandwich. Well-made sandwiches contain all five food groups. Calories are minimized yet energy is maximized for the calories consumed because complex carbohydrate (bread, crackers, vegetables, etc.) + protein (meat, cheese, fish, etc.) has a synergistic effect. Together they provide more staying power and fuel the body more efficiently than carbohydrate alone (even though both carbohydrate and protein contain four calories per gram). This balance of protein, carbohydrate, and limited fat is the basis of a diabetic diet, well known by health care professionals as a healthy, effective approach to losing weight.

With today's low-fat and nonfat foods, sandwiches are the perfect weight loss tool: gratifying, convenient, nutrient dense, and, of course, delicious. Today there is a vast array of healthy food choices available. Grocery shelves stock light, high-fiber breads with just 35 calories per slice! We can indulge and never feel deprived, using foods that once were "off limits." Now we can be generous with (fat-free) sour cream, mayonnaise, cottage cheese, salad dressings, even Cheddar and mozzarella cheese. Complex carbohydrates and lean protein naturally combine to make a practical, creative, and inexpensive weight-loss strategy.

Sandwiches Are Nutritious Fast-Food

Custom made for an accelerated lifestyle, sandwiches are nutritious fast-food that's portable and easy to eat on the run. Sandwiches can be prepared in advance and prepackaged for a fraction of the cost of restaurant meals. Make several now; freeze, then pull them out in the morning. By noon they will have thawed and be ready to stuff with lettuce, sprouts, or other vegetables. (See Chapter 3.)

These recipes include modified old-fashioned favorites such as the Skinny Bologna or the Tuna Hawaiian sandwich, which happily mingles the refreshing flavors of pineapple, coconut, and yogurt. Tuna is further transformed into Tex-Mex in the Don't Mess with Texas Beef Roll.

Refreshingly new flavor combinations include Spiced Pemmican Buns made with venison or other meats combined with raisins, apples, and spices. Fruitwiches team fresh fruit with ricotta cheese and nuts. Goat's cheese and mint marry within a folded over corn tortilla, and simple cheese bread with vegetables and herbed sour cream turn around one's conventional ideas of what a sandwich should be.

Keeping the Flavor In and the Fat Out

Fat is flavor. These recipes include several methods for intensifying the flavor in sandwiches without the fat through plentiful use of vegetables, fruits, low-fat meats, fish and cheese, spreads and condiments. Here are a few ideas:

Dip French toast in whipped egg white and bake for a souffle-like confection. Wrap fillings in romaine lettuce leaves, single sheets of phyllo dough, rice paper, or corn tortillas. Roast peppers for a husky flavor and stuff into vegetarian sandwiches. "Deep-fry" for a light crust by wrapping sandwich in a moist paper towel and microwaving one to two minutes.

Add "heat" with jalapeño peppers, horseradish, or ginger. Experiment with spices, fresh herbs, frozen concentrated fruit juices, and purees to flavor yogurt and sauces. Coarsely ground black pepper and cooked mushrooms render an earthiness. So does eggplant. Use the sharpness of lemon juice or vinegar to wake up bland foods. Harness the power of these natural condiments, and transform blander foods such as turkey, tofu, and fat-free yogurt.

Guidelines for Nutritional Data

All recipes are low in fat, not exceeding the 30 percent of calories-from-fat guideline recommended by the American Heart Association. Ninety-eight percent of the recipes are low in sodium, which translates to 600 mg or less per serving. It should be noted, however, that these guidelines represent food eaten over an entire day; thus any one particular food high in fat, such as ice cream, can be balanced with foods very low in fat, such as vegetables.

Each recipe includes a nutritional analysis, detailing calories and fat, cholesterol, sodium, protein, carbohydrate, and diabetic exchanges. Please understand that the nutritional data are not infallible but simply guidelines. They were developed with the following in mind:

1. Condiments were chosen with respect to keeping within fat and sodium guidelines. For your own personal taste, feel free to modify with higher-fat or sodium condiments, and balance as you will throughout the data to meet your own guidelines.

2. Where alternative ingredients or amounts are listed, the first ingredient or amount was used in our calculations.

3. Optional ingredients, garnishes, and items "to taste" were not figured into the nutritional data.

4. Although every effort was made to provide accurate data, types of breads, specific brands, and other variables make it impossible to assure total accuracy.

Use this book for ideas to fill a lunchbox, a child, or to prepare something simple and delicious for supper. Sandwich your life with emotional support, nutritious food, and alternating physical activity and relaxation. The result may be natural weight control, stress-free.

1.
BREAKFAST
SANDWICHES

J ust as high-octane fuel powers a finely tuned race car, nutritious breakfast food powers your strength and energy for the day. Simple sugars such as doughnuts, pancakes with syrup, croissants, and pastries shoot instant energy into the bloodstream, producing a sugar "high."

Insulin takes up the extra sugar in the bloodstream, resulting in a sudden drop of energy, and we may well become hungry, anxious, and moody by mid-morning. We can avoid these mood swings simply by eating balanced meals and snacks at regular intervals. For optimum mental and physical balance, plan for 55–60 percent of calories to come from carbohydrates, 15–20 percent from protein, and 20–30 percent from fat.

COUNTRY EGG AND GREEN ONION SANDWICH

This simple, unsophisticated sandwich, fit for a busy mom or a lazy day, can be put together in the time it takes to brush the mud off your shoes. Use the best coarse-grained bread you can find (it's more like home-made) and a fresh egg, if possible. This sandwich is wonderfully messy to eat. Don't forget to wipe the plate with your crust.

Serves 1

  Butter-flavored vegetable cooking spray
1 large egg
  Salt and pepper, to taste
2 slices coarse-grained, *or* homemade, wheat
  bread
1 green onion with top, chopped
1 teaspoon chili sauce

1. Coat an 8-in. nonstick skillet with vegetable spray. Fry the fresh egg slowly, covered. The egg white ideally will remain delicate and the yolk runny. Season with salt and pepper. Remove egg and wipe out pan.

2. Spray skillet again. Fry slices of bread until golden. Slip egg on one slice and cover generously with finely chopped green onions. Dot chili sauce over onions. Cover with second slice of bread.

Nutritional Data

PER SERVING		EXCHANGES	
Calories:	216	Milk:	0.0
% Calories from fat:	29	Vegetable:	0.0
Fat (gm):	7.1	Fruit:	0.0
Sat. fat (gm):	2	Bread:	1.6
Cholesterol (mg):	210	Meat:	0.9
Sodium (mg):	329	Fat:	0.9
Protein (gm):	11.1		
Carbohydrate (gm):	26.6		

A RICH MAN'S BREAKFAST

I once knew a man who ate caviar every morning for breakfast. A ritual worthy of consideration, it seems to me, to toast the day with elegance as well as nutrition. Serve with frosted grapes.

Serves 1

2 slices of calorie-reduced whole-wheat bread, toasted, *or* 2 rye crispbread crackers
2 tablespoons nonfat sour cream
2 tablespoons caviar
1 hard-boiled egg white, sieved, for garnish

1. If using bread, toast and cut off crusts. Spoon sour cream over toast (or crispbread) and place on a chilled plate. Spoon caviar over top. Garnish with egg white.

Nutritional Data

PER SERVING		EXCHANGES	
Calories:	181	Milk:	0.1
% Calories from fat:	28	Vegetable:	0.0
Fat (gm):	5	Fruit:	0.0
Sat. fat (gm):	1.3	Bread:	1.0
Cholesterol (mg):	188	Meat:	1.5
Sodium (mg):	597	Fat:	0.4
Protein (gm):	14		
Carbohydrate (gm):	19.5		

Breakfast Baked Alaska

Serves 2

2 egg whites
Dash cream of tartar, optional
1 tablespoon sugar
2/3 cup 2% low-fat cottage cheese
2 tablespoons raspberry no-sugar-added jam
1 English muffin, split

1. Preheat broiler.
2. Crack egg whites into a small metal bowl. Beat whites until soft peaks form. Add cream of tartar and sugar, 1 teaspoon at a time. Continue to beat until whites are stiff but not dry.
3. In a small bowl, combine cottage cheese and jam. Pack half of mixture into a 1/3 cup dry measuring cup. Unmold onto English muffin half. Spoon half of the whipped egg white over cottage cheese and jam. Repeat with other "Alaska." Set on pie plate and broil until egg whites are lightly brown, 1 to 2 minutes. Serve immediately.

Variation: Substitute nonfat frozen yogurt for cottage cheese and jam. Freeze yogurt in two 1/2-cup portions and unmold onto muffin halves. Follow recipe to completion.

Nutritional Data

PER SERVING		EXCHANGES	
Calories:	184	Milk:	0.0
% Calories from fat:	10	Vegetable:	0.0
Fat (gm):	1.9	Fruit:	0.5
Sat. fat (gm):	0.9	Bread:	0.8
Cholesterol (mg):	6.2	Meat:	2.0
Sodium (mg):	490	Fat:	0.1
Protein (gm):	16		
Carbohydrate (gm):	24.4		

SALSA BEEF CAKES

Serves 2

1/2 cup nonfat ricotta cheese
1/2 cup salsa
2 calorie-reduced hamburger buns, toasted
Vegetable cooking spray
2 2-oz. frozen beef steaks, thawed
Onion salt and black pepper, to taste

1. Combine ricotta cheese with salsa and mix well. Spread half of mixture over bottom of each bun.

2. Coat an 8-in. skillet with nonstick vegetable spray. Slowly saute beef steaks over medium heat. Season with onion salt and pepper. Turn and cook other side to desired doneness. Place on buns and serve hot with additional salsa, if desired.

Nutritional Data

PER SERVING		EXCHANGES	
Calories:	232	Milk:	0.4
% Calories from fat:	27	Vegetable:	0.0
Fat (gm):	6.9	Fruit:	0.0
Sat. fat (gm):	2.1	Bread:	0.5
Cholesterol (mg):	41.1	Meat:	1.7
Sodium (mg):	595	Fat:	0.1
Protein (gm):	24.5		
Carbohydrate (gm):	18.1		

FRUIT DANISH

*Nonfat ricotta cheese, jam, and almonds embellish an English muffin—
a nutritious breakfast and a good way to spoil oneself.*

Serves 2

1 English muffin, split
2 tablespoons sliced almonds
½ cup nonfat ricotta cheese
¼ cup nonfat sour cream
2 tablespoons no-sugar-added jam, *or* jelly—your
  favorite flavor

1. Toast English muffin halves and place on individual plates.

2. Preheat broiler. Sprinkle almonds onto a pie plate and set under broiler 1 to 3 minutes. Watch almonds carefully; they don't take much time and quickly burn!

3. Combine ricotta with sour cream and smear half of mixture over each English muffin, making a slight indentation in the center with a spoon. Spoon jam into center, and sprinkle with toasted almonds.

Nutritional Data

PER SERVING		EXCHANGES	
Calories:	204	Milk:	0.8
% Calories from fat:	18	Vegetable:	0.0
Fat (gm):	4.2	Fruit:	0.5
Sat. fat (gm):	Trace	Bread:	0.8
Cholesterol (mg):	6	Meat:	0.8
Sodium (mg):	201	Fat:	0.9
Protein (gm):	15.5		
Carbohydrate (gm):	29.3		

New Mexican Egg Tostadas

Just one teaspoon of red chili sauce supplies a full day's requirement of vitamin A.

Serves 2

2 whole-wheat tortillas (8 in.)
Vegetable cooking spray
½ cup nonfat refried beans
1 green onion, thinly sliced
2 eggs
Red Sauce (recipe follows)
2 tablespoons nonfat sour cream
Fresh cilantro leaves, for garnish

1. Preheat oven to 450 degrees. To crisp tortillas: immerse in water; drain. Coat a 10 x 15-in. cookie sheet with nonstick spray and place tortillas on it. Bake 2 to 3 minutes or until lightly golden.

2. Turn oven down to 350 degrees. Remove tortillas from oven and spoon a thin ring of refried beans around outer edge of each. Sprinkle green onions evenly over beans. Break an egg into center of each tortilla. Return pan to oven and bake until eggs are set, 15 to 20 minutes.

3. Carefully loosen tortillas from pan with a wide spatula. Transfer a tostada to each plate. Pour Red Sauce around edges. Serve with sour cream. Garnish with cilantro leaves, if desired.

Red Sauce

½ cup chopped onion
1 cup low-sodium beef broth
2 ozs. dried red chili pods (½ cup crushed)

1. In a covered saucepan, combine chopped onions and beef broth. Simmer over medium heat until onions are soft, 5 to 8 minutes.

2. Break tops off chili pods and discard. Shake free the loose seeds. (Keep a few if you like it hot.) Fill blender with all ingredients and process just until smooth.

Nutritional Data

PER SERVING		EXCHANGES	
Calories:	249	Milk:	0.1
% Calories from fat:	27	Vegetable:	0.2
Fat (gm):	7.6	Fruit:	0.0
Sat. fat (gm):	1.9	Bread:	1.7
Cholesterol (mg):	210	Meat:	1.0
Sodium (mg):	424	Fat:	1.0
Protein (gm):	13.9		
Carbohydrate (gm):	32.1		

FARMER'S BREAKFAST SANDWICH

My sister and I had scrambled eggs over buttered toast every chilly Michigan morning (which seemed to be about 300 days a year). Back then, we didn't have tofu, yet this version brings me back to that buttery, rich-tasting breakfast that is now my comfort food.

Serves 2

  5 ozs. extra-light tofu
  1/2 cup egg substitute
  2 tablespoons skimmed evaporated milk
  1 1/2 tablespoons bacon bits
  1 tablespoon chopped parsley
  Vegetable cooking spray
  1/4 cup finely chopped onion
  1/2 cup chopped mushrooms
  Freshly ground black pepper
  4 slices calorie-reduced whole-wheat bread, toasted
  1 1/2 tablespoons diet margarine, divided

1. In a medium bowl, break up tofu with a fork. Add and beat in the egg substitute, evaporated milk, bacon bits, and parsley; set aside.

2. Coat an 8-in. nonstick skillet with vegetable spray and saute onions and mushrooms over medium heat until soft. Stir in tofu mixture and

season with pepper. Cook over low heat, stirring occasionally, until mixture resembles scrambled eggs.

3. Over 2 slices of toast, spread margarine and place on individual plates. Divide tofu mixture and spread over toast. Cover with top slice of toast.

Nutritional Data

PER SERVING		EXCHANGES	
Calories:	230	Milk:	0.2
% Calories from fat:	28	Vegetable:	0.4
Fat (gm):	7.5	Fruit:	0.0
Sat. fat (gm):	1.2	Bread:	1.4
Cholesterol (mg):	0.5	Meat:	1.4
Sodium (mg):	593	Fat:	1.0
Protein (gm):	17.3		
Carbohydrate (gm):	27.5		

EGGS IN A CUMULUS CLOUD

Serves 2

1 pumpernickel bagel, split, lightly toasted
4 teaspoons nonfat cream cheese
2 egg whites, stiffly beaten
1 egg yolk
  Paprika, to taste
  Black pepper, to taste
  Parsley sprigs, for garnish

1. Preheat broiler.

2. Spread toasted bagel with cream cheese.

3. Spoon egg white completely over bagel halves, covering hole. Make a well in center of egg white and divide yolk into holes. Set under broiler and broil until egg white is lightly golden.

4. Season with paprika and pepper to taste. Garnish with parsley.

Nutritional Data

PER SERVING		EXCHANGES	
Calories:	184	Milk:	0.1
% Calories from fat:	29	Vegetable:	0.0
Fat (gm):	5.6	Fruit:	0.0
Sat. fat (gm):	1.6	Bread:	1.3
Cholesterol (mg):	212	Meat:	0.9
Sodium (mg):	338	Fat:	0.6
Protein (gm):	12.1		
Carbohydrate (gm):	19.5		

EGGS IN HELL

Here is a hair of the dog that may have bitten you: a hangover remedy.
Perfect as a late-night breakfast.

Serves 2

1 cup low-sodium vegetable juice cocktail
4 drops hot pepper sauce, such as Tabasco
1 teaspoon yeast extract, such as Vegemite, *or* 1
   teaspoon Worcestershire sauce
2 eggs
1/4 cup light beer
2 slices wheat bran bread, toasted
   Chopped parsley, *or* cilantro, for garnish

1. In an 8-in. nonstick skillet, bring juice, hot pepper sauce, and yeast extract (or Worcestershire sauce) to a slow simmer. Reduce heat.

2. Carefully break eggs into a saucer and slip them into sauce. Cook slowly, spooning sauce over egg yolks. When eggs are done to your liking, pour beer over eggs. Simmer just until beer is warm.

3. With a spatula, lift each egg out of sauce; drain. Place on toast. Garnish with chopped parsley or cilantro.

Nutritional Data

PER SERVING		EXCHANGES	
Calories:	200	Milk:	0.0
% Calories from fat:	28	Vegetable:	1.0
Fat (gm):	6.3	Fruit:	0.0
Sat. fat (gm):	1.8	Bread:	1.1
Cholesterol (mg):	210	Meat:	0.9
Sodium (mg):	291	Fat:	0.7
Protein (gm):	10.7		
Carbohydrate (gm):	23.6		

FRENCH APPLE-SAUSAGE SANDWICH

For extra decadence, drink caffè latte with this dish.

Serves 6

Butter-flavored vegetable cooking spray
1 cup finely chopped Granny Smith apple
¼ cup wheat bran
1 teaspoon each: garlic salt, white pepper, all-spice, ginger, nutmeg, and cinnamon
1 lb. lean ground chicken breast, *or* turkey breast
6 slices raisin bread, toasted
Paper doily
Powdered sugar
Fruit, such as strawberries, for garnish

1. Coat a 6 to 8-in. saute pan with vegetable spray. Over medium heat, saute apples until soft, stirring occasionally.

2. Combine wheat bran and all spices in a medium bowl; swirl to combine. Mix in ground chicken with your hands. Fold in apples.

3. Divide sausage mixture into 6 equal parts (with floured hands, if necessary). Shape into patties and saute in a medium saute pan coated with nonstick spray. Cook until brown; flip and cook other side until cooked through, 8 to 10 minutes. Drain on paper towels.

4. Place 1 sausage patty on top of raisin toast slices. Place a small, round paper doily over sausage. Sift powdered sugar over top and remove doily. Garnish with fruit, if desired.

Nutritional Data

PER SERVING		EXCHANGES	
Calories:	242	Milk:	0.0
% Calories from fat:	27	Vegetable:	0.0
Fat (gm):	6.9	Fruit:	1.1
Sat. fat (gm):	2.2	Bread:	0.9
Cholesterol (mg):	59.7	Meat:	1.8
Sodium (mg):	535	Fat:	0.3
Protein (gm):	16.4		
Carbohydrate (gm):	33.5		

STRAWBERRY-CHEESE SHORTCAKE

Serves 2

1 English muffin, split
3 tablespoons nonfat cream cheese
1 cup sliced strawberries
4 tablespoons light whipped cream, pressurized
  or frozen, thawed
1 tablespoon thinly sliced almonds

1. Toast English muffin halves under light setting in toaster.

2. Spread cream cheese over muffin halves. Spoon half of strawberries over each muffin. Spray or spoon whipped cream over all and sprinkle with almonds.

Nutritional Data

PER SERVING		EXCHANGES	
Calories:	136	Milk:	0.2
% Calories from fat:	30	Vegetable:	0.0
Fat (gm):	4.4	Fruit:	0.0
Sat. fat (gm):	1.9	Bread:	0.8
Cholesterol (mg):	3.7	Meat:	0.0
Sodium (mg):	266	Fat:	0.9
Protein (gm):	6.2		
Carbohydrate (gm):	17.2		

STRAWBERRY FRENCH TOAST

Serves 2

½ cup egg substitute
½ cup strawberry nectar
2 slices day-old French bread
Vegetable cooking spray
1 cup Winter Strawberry Sauce (recipe follows),
or sliced strawberries
Confectioner's sugar, optional

1. Combine egg substitute and strawberry nectar in a shallow bowl. Submerse bread into mixture, covering and coating both sides.

2. Coat a 10-in. nonstick skillet with vegetable spray and bring to medium heat. Saute French toast until lightly brown; flip and cook other side until done. Transfer to serving plate. Serve topped with Winter Strawberry Sauce or sliced strawberries. Sift confectioner's sugar over toast for a pretty touch.

Nutritional Data *(including Winter Strawberry Sauce)*

PER SERVING		EXCHANGES	
Calories:	138	Milk:	0.0
% Calories from fat:	6	Vegetable:	0.0
Fat (gm):	1	Fruit:	1.9
Sat. fat (gm):	0.2	Bread:	0.9
Cholesterol (mg):	0	Meat:	0.5
Sodium (mg):	214	Fat:	0.1
Protein (gm):	6.4		
Carbohydrate (gm):	25.8		

Winter Strawberry Sauce
Makes 1½ cups

1   11½-oz. can strawberry nectar
1   tablespoon cornstarch
1   tablespoon apple juice concentrate, thawed

1. In a 2-cup measure, combine nectar, cornstarch, and apple juice concentrate. Microwave (high) 1½ to 2 minutes or until syrup is clear and thickened, stirring once a minute during cooking. Excess sauce will keep, refrigerated, up to 1 week.

Nutritional Data

PER ½-CUP SERVING		EXCHANGES	
Calories:	89	Milk:	0.0
% Calories from fat:	0	Vegetable:	0.0
Fat (gm):	0	Fruit:	4.0
Sat. fat (gm):	0	Bread:	0.2
Cholesterol (mg):	0	Meat:	0.0
Sodium (mg):	3.5	Fat:	0.0
Protein (gm):	0.1		
Carbohydrate (gm):	22		

EGG IN A BISCUIT

Serves 1

1 large shredded wheat biscuit
Vegetable cooking spray
1 large egg
Herbal blend, light salt, pepper, and/or butter-
flavored sprinkles, to taste

1. Hold biscuit under running water and carefully flatten biscuit.
2. Coat an 8-in. nonstick skillet with vegetable spray. Saute biscuit over medium heat 3 to 4 minutes or until golden.
3. Crack egg over biscuit. Break yolk, if desired. Cover and cook over low heat until egg is set. Season with herbal blend, light salt, pepper, and butter-flavored sprinkles, to taste.

Nutritional Data

PER SERVING		EXCHANGES	
Calories:	154	Milk:	0.0
% Calories from fat:	27	Vegetable:	1.0
Fat (gm):	5.1	Fruit:	0.0
Sat. fat (gm):	1.6	Bread:	1.0
Cholesterol (mg):	210	Meat:	0.9
Sodium (mg):	63	Fat:	0.5
Protein (gm):	11.3		
Carbohydrate (gm):	19		

RASPBERRY BROIL

Hot, sweet, and savory. In place of homemade bread, use frozen loaves or hot roll mix. Better yet, obtain a bread baking machine. The comforting results are worth the expense.

Serves 1

1 thick slice (2 ozs.) homemade white bread, toasted
1 tablespoon reduced-fat peanut butter, chunky or plain
2 teaspoons reduced-calorie raspberry preserves

1. Preheat broiler.
2. Spread 1 tablespoon peanut butter on bread. Top with reduced-calorie raspberry preserves.
3. Place on piece of foil or in broiler pan. Broil until preserve is bubbly.

Nutritional Data

PER SERVING		EXCHANGES	
Calories:	241	Milk:	0.0
% Calories from fat:	28	Vegetable:	0.0
Fat (gm):	7.5	Fruit:	0.3
Sat. fat (gm):	1.5	Bread:	2.6
Cholesterol (mg):	3	Meat:	0.0
Sodium (mg):	253	Fat:	1.5
Protein (gm):	7.1		
Carbohydrate (gm):	36.5		

PEANUT BUTTER SPICED BAGELS

Serves 4

2 tablespoons reduced-fat crunchy peanut butter
4 ozs. (8 tablespoons) nonfat cream cheese
1 teaspoon vanilla
2 teaspoons brown sugar
1/2 teaspoon ground allspice
2 plain bagels, split and toasted

1. In a small bowl (a wooden bowl works well), using a wooden spoon, blend together peanut butter, cream cheese, vanilla, brown sugar, and allspice.

2. Spread peanut butter mixture over each bagel half, pop in toaster oven, and broil until lightly browned.

Nutritional Data

PER SERVING		EXCHANGES	
Calories:	166	Milk:	0.1
% Calories from fat:	19	Vegetable:	0.0
Fat (gm):	3.6	Fruit:	0.0
Sat. fat (gm):	0.5	Bread:	1.9
Cholesterol (mg):	2.5	Meat:	0.0
Sodium (mg):	237	Fat:	0.7
Protein (gm):	7.5		
Carbohydrate (gm):	26.1		

EGGS BENEDICT TARRAGON

Serves 4

3 tablespoons tarragon vinegar
3 sprigs fresh tarragon, *or* ¼ teaspoon dried tarragon
4 large eggs
2 English muffins, split and toasted
2 tablespoons Lemon Tarragon Sauce (recipe follows)

1. Fill a 10 to 12-in. skillet with 3 cups water or enough to make a poaching bath at least 1-in. deep. Add vinegar and tarragon. Bring to a simmer over medium-low heat.

2. Break each egg into a small cup, then carefully slide each into the tarragon water. Simmer gently about 2 minutes or until whites are set, spooning the hot liquid over eggs to lightly film yolks. Using a slotted spoon remove eggs and drain. Place on English muffin halves. Spoon on Lemon Tarragon Sauce.

Lemon Tarragon Sauce

½ cup nonfat plain yogurt
2 teaspoons grated lemon rind
   Pinch of fresh, *or* dried, tarragon
   Parsley leaf, optional

1. Combine yogurt with lemon rind and a pinch of tarragon. Spoon 2 tablespoons over each egg. Garnish with fresh parsley or tarragon.

Nutritional Data

PER SERVING		EXCHANGES	
Calories:	173	Milk:	0.4
% Calories from fat:	29	Vegetable:	0.0
Fat (gm):	5.6	Fruit:	0.0
Sat. fat (gm):	1.6	Bread:	0.8
Cholesterol (mg):	211	Meat:	0.9
Sodium (mg):	236	Fat:	0.6
Protein (gm):	11.8		
Carbohydrate (gm):	18.3		

BREAKFAST IN A TORTILLA

You'll have all five food groups in one lean "sandwich."

Serves 6

1 16-oz. can fruit cocktail in juice
6 corn tortillas
  Vegetable cooking spray
1½ cups egg substitute
1 cup sliced green onions
1½ cups shredded nonfat Cheddar cheese
6 1-in. slices turkey bacon, fried crisp and
  drained

1. Drain fruit cocktail, reserving ⅓ cup liquid. Crisp tortillas in microwave by placing between 2 paper towels. Cook (high) 1 minute or until crisp.

2. Combine egg substitute with reserved fruit cocktail liquid and beat until fluffy. Coat a nonstick 8-in. skillet with vegetable spray. Scramble egg substitute over low heat until soft. Stir in green onions.

3. Spoon eggs over tortillas and sprinkle with cheese. Crumble a strip of bacon and sprinkle it over top. Repeat with remaining strips of bacon.

Nutritional Data

PER SERVING		EXCHANGES	
Calories:	200	Milk:	0.1
% Calories from fat:	14	Vegetable:	0.0
Fat (gm):	3.1	Fruit:	0.7
Sat. fat (gm):	1.5	Bread:	0.8
Cholesterol (mg):	25	Meat:	2.5
Sodium (mg):	525	Fat:	0.3
Protein (gm):	20		
Carbohydrate (gm):	23.6		

TROPICAL TOAST

Nice to serve for breakfast in bed. Make toast ahead, refrigerate, then bake in the morning. This might also be a good time to get out those island travel brochures and plan a dream of yours.

Serves 4

- 3/4 cup egg substitute
- 3/4 cup orange juice
- 3 tablespoons lime juice
- 1/4 cup powdered sugar
- 1/2 teaspoon coconut extract
- 8 slices Hawaiian, *or* French, bread (cut diagonally from loaf), each about 1/2-in. thick
- 3/4 cup unsweetened flaked coconut, divided
- 1 kiwi, sliced, for garnish
- 1/2 cup chunk pineapple in juice, drained, for garnish

1. Preheat oven to 400 degrees.

2. In a wide bowl, beat together egg substitute, orange juice, lime juice, powdered sugar, and coconut extract until well blended.

3. Dip each piece of bread in egg mixture, turning to saturate both sides. Arrange slices in a single layer on lightly greased 12 x 15-in. baking sheet. Sprinkle tops of slices evenly with half the coconut. With spatula, lightly press coconut into bread.

4. Bake bread until coconut is lightly browned, about 10 minutes. With a wide spatula, turn slices over. Sprinkle evenly with remaining coconut. Continue baking until slices are puffed and coconut and bread are lightly browned, about 10 minutes longer.

5. Transfer slices to individual plates, 2 per serving. Garnish with kiwi and pineapple chunks.

Nutritional Data

PER SERVING		EXCHANGES	
Calories:	161	Milk:	0.0
% Calories from fat:	22	Vegetable:	0.0
Fat (gm):	3.9	Fruit:	0.4
Sat. fat (gm):	2.9	Bread:	0.9
Cholesterol (mg):	0	Meat:	0.3
Sodium (mg):	205	Fat:	0.7
Protein (gm):	4.7		
Carbohydrate (gm):	27.5		

ROAST BEEF PASTIES

Make hot pocket sandwiches the night before from leftovers. Tender and flaky, this upscale sandwich can be eaten on the run.

Serves 5

Vegetable cooking spray
1/2 medium onion, sliced
2 cups sliced mushrooms
2 tablespoons dry red wine
6 ozs. lean roast beef, shredded
1/4 teaspoon garlic powder
Pinch coarsely ground black pepper
1 pkg. (7 1/2 ozs., 10 biscuits) refrigerated biscuits
3 tablespoons 1% low-fat milk
1 tablespoon sesame seeds

1. Coat a medium skillet with vegetable spray. Over medium-low heat, saute onions 2 to 3 minutes. Add mushrooms, wine, and beef. Season with garlic powder and pepper. Continue to cook until mushrooms are soft and mixture is cooked through.

2. On a floured surface, roll each biscuit into a 5-in. circle. Place 1/3 cup of filling on each dough round; moisten dough edges with water. Cover with remaining dough rounds. Press edges together with your fingers, making a fluted edge.

3. Brush tops with milk; sprinkle with sesame seeds. Place pasties on ungreased baking sheet. Bake in 450-degree oven 15 minutes or until golden brown. Cool on wire rack.

Nutritional Data

PER SERVING		EXCHANGES	
Calories:	199	Milk:	0.0
% Calories from fat:	26	Vegetable:	0.5
Fat (gm):	5.8	Fruit:	0.0
Sat. fat (gm):	1.1	Bread:	1.4
Cholesterol (mg):	25.7	Meat:	1.4
Sodium (mg):	390	Fat:	0.6
Protein (gm):	13.6		
Carbohydrate (gm):	23.6		

WAYNE'S CHILI HONEY MUFFINS

Red chili honey is a specialty of New Mexico. It is made from the honey of wildflowers combined with ground chili powder. Make it yourself with this recipe.

Serves 1

  1 tablespoon mild-flavored honey
  ½ teaspoon New Mexican ground chili
  4 teaspoons whipped cream cheese
  1 English muffin, split and lightly toasted

1. Stir in honey and chili together.
2. Spread cream cheese over toasted muffins. Lavish on the chili honey and serve warm.

Nutritional Data

PER SERVING		EXCHANGES	
Calories:	248	Milk:	0.1
% Calories from fat:	26	Vegetable:	0.0
Fat (gm):	7	Fruit:	0.0
Sat. fat (gm):	4.1	Bread:	1.7
Cholesterol (mg):	20	Meat:	0.1
Sodium (mg):	323	Fat:	1.5
Protein (gm):	5.8		
Carbohydrate (gm):	40.9		

Hot Gingerbread Toasties

Four ounces of tofu have more protein than an egg!

Serves 2

1 cup soft-medium tofu
2 teaspoons brown sugar
1/2 teaspoon apple pie spice
1/2 teaspoon instant coffee
1/2 teaspoon ginger
2 slices pumpernickel, *or* whole-wheat, bread, toasted

1. Preheat broiler.
2. Drain tofu and press free of water. Using a wooden spoon, blend together the first 5 ingredients and spread over slices of toast. Broil until brown, bubbly, and delicious.

Nutritional Data

PER SERVING

		EXCHANGES	
Calories:	245	Milk:	0.0
% Calories from fat:	22	Vegetable:	0.0
Fat (gm):	6.2	Fruit:	0.0
Sat. fat (gm):	1	Bread:	2.2
Cholesterol (mg):	0	Meat:	1.2
Sodium (mg):	277	Fat:	2.9
Protein (gm):	11.6		
Carbohydrate (gm):	36.5		

Coconut Rum Toast

Serves 2

4 tablespoons nonfat sour cream
2 tablespoons nonfat milk
2 tablespoons shredded coconut

1   tablespoon light brown sugar
1/8 teaspoon each: vanilla and rum extracts
2   slices raisin bread, toasted

1. Blend together sour cream, milk, coconut, brown sugar, and extracts.

2. Spread half of mixture over each slice of toast, covering entire surface. Transfer toast to nonstick baking sheet and broil 3 inches from heat source until heated through, about 1 minute.

3. Cut each slice diagonally and serve immediately.

Nutritional Data

PER SERVING		EXCHANGES	
Calories:	239	Milk:	0.3
% Calories from fat:	24	Vegetable:	0.0
Fat (gm):	6.6	Fruit:	0.0
Sat. fat (gm):	4.4	Bread:	1.8
Cholesterol (mg):	1.2	Meat:	0.0
Sodium (mg):	268	Fat:	1.3
Protein (gm):	7.6		
Carbohydrate (gm):	39.4		

BREAKFAST BURRITOS

Serves 6

Vegetable cooking spray
1   cup sliced mushrooms
2   6-oz. cans no-salt vegetable juice, divided
1   tablespoon cornstarch
    Hot pepper sauce, to taste
2   cups shredded chicken breast
1/4 cup chopped green onion
3/4 cup egg substitute
3   tablespoons nonfat milk
6   whole-wheat tortillas (6 in.)
2   tablespoons Parmesan cheese
    Fresh parsley, *or* cilantro, chopped, for garnish

1. Coat medium saucepan with nonstick spray and place over medium heat. Saute mushrooms 2 minutes, stirring occasionally.

2. Stir cornstarch into ¼ cup of vegetable juice until dissolved; add mixture to mushrooms in pan. Add remaining juice, stirring constantly until sauce thickens; season with hot pepper sauce, then set aside.

3. Meanwhile, coat a medium skillet with vegetable spray. Stir-fry chicken and green onions over medium heat 4 to 5 minutes.

4. In a small bowl, beat egg substitute with milk and pour into the stir-fry; reduce heat to low. As eggs begin to set, lift them with a spatula to allow uncooked egg to flow to bottom. Cook until eggs are almost set but still moist.

5. Spoon egg and chicken mixture along center of each tortilla, dividing mixture evenly. Fold one edge over the filling and carefully roll up.

6. Coat a 9 x 13-in. baking dish with vegetable spray. Arrange tortillas in dish. Pour reserved vegetable juice and mushrooms mixture over tortillas and sprinkle with Parmesan cheese. Bake at 375 degrees for 10 minutes or until hot and bubbly. Garnish with chopped parsley.

Nutritional Data

PER SERVING		EXCHANGES	
Calories:	240	Milk:	0.0
% Calories from fat:	21	Vegetable:	0.5
Fat (gm):	5.3	Fruit:	0.0
Sat. fat (gm):	1.4	Bread:	1.4
Cholesterol (mg):	41	Meat:	2.5
Sodium (mg):	301	Fat:	0.6
Protein (gm):	21.7		
Carbohydrate (gm):	25		

WAFFLED CHICKEN IN A BISCUIT

Serves 5

Vegetable cooking spray
4 tablespoons nonfat sour cream
2 tablespoons chopped green chilies
1 pkg. (7½ ozs., 10 biscuits) refrigerated biscuits
4 ozs. deli-sliced oven-roasted chicken breast
1 small tomato, thinly sliced

1. Coat waffle iron with vegetable spray, and heat according to manufacturer's directions.

2. Combine sour cream and chilies in small bowl.

3. Spoon a tablespoon of sour cream mixture onto a biscuit and place in center of waffle iron. Layer a portion of chicken over biscuit, followed by thin slices of tomato. Cover with second biscuit and lower top of waffle iron. Press lid down slightly to flatten biscuit. Bake 2 to 4 minutes or until golden brown. Continue with remaining biscuits.

Nutritional Data

PER SERVING		EXCHANGES	
Calories:	140	Milk:	0.1
% Calories from fat:	17	Vegetable:	0.2
Fat (gm):	2.5	Fruit:	0.0
Sat. fat (gm):	0	Bread:	1.4
Cholesterol (mg):	21	Meat:	0.8
Sodium (mg):	587	Fat:	0.4
Protein (gm):	5.8		
Carbohydrate (gm):	21.8		

CRUNCHY FRENCH TOAST SANDWICH

For very low-sodium diets, opt for low-sodium corn flakes (only 2 milligrams of sodium per cup) instead of regular corn flakes with a whopping 277 milligrams!

Serves 2

Vegetable cooking spray
1/4 cup egg substitute
3/4 cup skim milk
1 teaspoon vanilla extract
1 cup low-sodium corn flakes, crushed
1 teaspoon cinnamon
2 teaspoons sugar
2/3 cup nonfat cottage cheese
1/4 cup fresh, *or* frozen, blueberries

2 teaspoons grated lemon rind
4 slices day-old calorie-reduced, white bread
Confectioner's sugar, for garnish

1. Preheat oven to 450 degrees. Coat an 8 x 8 x 2-in. baking pan with vegetable spray.

2. In small mixing bowl, beat together egg substitute, skim milk, and vanilla. On sheet of wax paper, combine corn flake crumbs, cinnamon, and sugar.

3. Fold blueberries and lemon rind into cottage cheese. Spread over 2 slices of bread and cover with remaining slices.

4. Dip sandwich into egg mixture, then lightly into crumb mixture, coating both sides; repeat procedure with remaining sandwich. Arrange sandwiches in a single layer in prepared pan and bake, turning once, until crisp and lightly browned, about 10 minutes on each side. Sift confectioner's sugar over sandwiches.

Nutritional Data

PER SERVING		EXCHANGES	
Calories:	250	Milk:	0.2
% Calories from fat:	7	Vegetable:	0.0
Fat (gm):	2	Fruit:	0.2
Sat. fat (gm):	0.6	Bread:	2.5
Cholesterol (mg):	45	Meat:	1.8
Sodium (mg):	481	Fat:	0.3
Protein (gm):	19.1		
Carbohydrate (gm):	42.1		

COMMUTING OMELET

Crackerbread (a high-fiber cracker) can be transformed with a little moisture into a soft and chewy bread, much like that of an ice cream sandwich. Prepare these the night before, toss into your briefcase, and breakfast in the comfort of freeway traffic or on your spacious, uncluttered desk.

Serves 3

2 whole eggs + 4 egg whites, lightly beaten, *or* 1 cup egg substitute
2 tablespoons nonfat milk
1 cup sliced mushrooms
¼ cup fresh parsley, *or* cilantro, chopped
Black pepper, *or* your favorite seasoning, to taste
Butter-flavored vegetable cooking spray
6 high-fiber crackerbreads, such as Rye-Crisp or Extra Fiber WASA crispbread
Dijon-style mustard

1. With a wire whisk, beat eggs, egg whites, and milk. Add mushrooms and parsley (or cilantro) and pepper (or your favorite seasoning).

2. Coat an 8-in. omelet pan with vegetable spray. Prepare omelet, using egg mixture. Roll into a cylinder and cut in thirds.

3. Spread 3 crackerbreads with light coating of mustard. Tuck omelet portion between crackers, mustard side down. Wrap tightly in plastic wrap. Repeat with other sandwiches. Refrigerate at least 6 hours or overnight.

Nutritional Data

PER SERVING		EXCHANGES	
Calories:	161	Milk:	0.0
% Calories from fat:	23	Vegetable:	0.2
Fat (gm):	4	Fruit:	0.0
Sat. fat (gm):	1.1	Bread:	1.0
Cholesterol (mg):	140	Meat:	1.3
Sodium (mg):	268	Fat:	0.4
Protein (gm):	11.6		
Carbohydrate (gm):	18.7		

Orange Marmalade and Ham Sandwich

Get 200 percent of the recommended daily allowance of vitamin C and a solid energy boost from this sandwich!

Serves 2

3 tablespoons orange juice
1 egg
2 tablespoons nonfat ricotta cheese
4 tablespoons no-sugar-added orange marmalade
4 slices day-old, calorie-reduced whole-wheat, *or* oatmeal, bread
2 ozs. sliced lean boiled, *or* cooked, ham
  Vegetable cooking spray
  Confectioner's sugar, for garnish

1. Combine orange juice and egg in shallow bowl; beat with a wire whisk and set aside.

2. Spread 1 tablespoon ricotta cheese on each of two slices of bread and 2 tablespoons orange marmalade on remaining slices. Layer ham over cheese and cover with marmalade slices.

3. Coat a medium skillet with nonstick vegetable spray and place over medium heat. Dip each sandwich into egg mixture, coating well. Cook sandwiches 3 minutes on each side or until golden. Sift confectioner's sugar over sandwiches.

Nutritional Data

PER SERVING		EXCHANGES	
Calories:	202	Milk:	0.1
% Calories from fat:	19	Vegetable:	0.0
Fat (gm):	4.5	Fruit:	0.7
Sat. fat (gm):	1.3	Bread:	1.4
Cholesterol (mg):	121	Meat:	1.4
Sodium (mg):	499	Fat:	0.7
Protein (gm):	14.4		
Carbohydrate (gm):	29.5		

2.
TOPLESS SANDWICHES

Open-face sandwiches can be quite beautiful. They may be edible works of art, as are tostadas, imaginative pizzas, or even French toast topped with strawberries and powdered sugar. With a topless sandwich, use your creative license and see if it doesn't *taste* better.

This type of sandwich is also the most fun to eat and is a delightful way to extend the sensuality of food, adding a smidgen more of *this* and a tad more of *that*. Tear it apart and eat it in pieces or use a knife and fork for more delicacy and to make it last longer.

SEAFOOD SOUFFLE ON TOAST

Serves 3

   1 teaspoon diet margarine
   3 tablespoons minced shallots
   2 teaspoons all-purpose flour
 1/4 cup nonfat milk
   1 egg yolk
   1 tablespoon minced fresh tarragon
 1/8 teaspoon pepper
   2 egg whites
 1/2 cup shredded low-fat Cheddar cheese
   6 ozs. cooked lobster, *or* scallops (about
      1 1/4 cups)
   3 slices calorie-reduced sourdough bread
      Fresh tarragon, optional

1. Preheat oven to 450 degrees.

2. Slowly melt margarine in a small saucepan over low heat. Add shallots and saute 2 minutes. Add flour; cook 1 minute, stirring constantly with a wire whisk. Gradually add milk; cook until thickened and bubbly, stirring constantly. Remove from heat.

3. Add egg yolk, tarragon, and pepper, stirring well with a wire whisk; set aside.

4. Beat egg whites at high speed with an electric mixer until stiff peaks form. Gently fold egg whites and cheese into milk mixture.

5. Divide seafood in thirds and arrange on bread slices. Place on baking sheet. Spread egg mixture evenly over seafood. Bake 5 minutes or until lightly browned. Garnish with tarragon or parsley, if desired.

Nutritional Data

PER SERVING		EXCHANGES	
Calories:	208	Milk:	0.1
% Calories from fat:	29	Vegetable:	0.0
Fat (gm):	6.8	Fruit:	0.0
Sat. fat (gm):	2.9	Bread:	0.8
Cholesterol (mg):	125	Meat:	1.9
Sodium (mg):	533	Fat:	0.4
Protein (gm):	23.8		
Carbohydrate (gm):	14.1		

SPRINGTIME OPEN FACE

Goat's cheese imparts earthiness and asparagus symbolizes new beginnings.

Serves 2

Vegetable cooking spray
1/2 cup egg substitute
2 slices whole-wheat bread, toasted
1 oz. (about 2 tablespoons) soft goat's cheese
6 cooked asparagus spears
2 1-oz. slices lean boiled, *or* cooked, ham
1 teaspoon fresh tarragon, *or* 1/2 teaspoon dried tarragon, crumbled
2 teaspoons freshly grated Parmesan cheese

1. Preheat broiler. Coat 2 individual ovenproof dishes with nonstick cooking spray.

2. Coat a small saute pan with nonstick vegetable spray and scramble egg substitute; set aside.

3. Spread half the goat's cheese over each slice of toast. Place each slice in an ovenproof dish. Top each with 3 asparagus spears, half the ham, and half the scrambled egg. Sprinkle tarragon and Parmesan over sandwiches. Broil until hot, 1 to 2 minutes.

Nutritional Data

PER SERVING		EXCHANGES	
Calories:	179	Milk:	0.0
% Calories from fat:	30	Vegetable:	0.1
Fat (gm):	6	Fruit:	0.0
Sat. fat (gm):	3	Bread:	0.8
Cholesterol (mg):	17	Meat:	2.1
Sodium (mg):	579	Fat:	0.6
Protein (gm):	17.2		
Carbohydrate (gm):	13.4		

FRENCH ONION SANDWICH

*This sandwich is like eating French onion soup
with a knife and fork.*

Serves 2

½ cup low-sodium beef broth
1 medium onion, sliced thinly
2 tablespoons dry white wine
2 slices calorie-reduced French bread, toasted
2 ozs. part-skim mozzarella cheese, shredded
(about ½ cup)
Black pepper

1. Coat a medium fry pan with nonstick spray. Simmer onions in beef broth, covered, over low heat until onions are limp and translucent, about 10 minutes. Just before onions are cooked, splash wine over them. Cook 1 minute more; remove from heat.
2. Place toast on 9 x 12-in. baking sheet. Pile onions over toast and sprinkle with shredded cheese. Broil until cheese melts.
3. Serve hot with plenty of freshly grated black pepper.

Nutritional Data

PER SERVING		EXCHANGES	
Calories:	157	Milk:	0.0
% Calories from fat:	14	Vegetable:	1.5
Fat (gm):	2.5	Fruit:	0.0
Sat. fat (gm):	1	Bread:	0.7
Cholesterol (mg):	8	Meat:	1.5
Sodium (mg):	198	Fat:	0.1
Protein (gm):	14.2		
Carbohydrate (gm):	21.2		

ZUCCHINI BROIL

Pile sauteed zucchini just as high as you like. Then, for éclat, garnish with some edible flower such as nasturtium, pansy, rose, or carnation.

Serves 2

½ cup minced onion
1 clove garlic, pressed
1 teaspoon fresh basil, crumbled, *or* ½ teaspoon dried
1 teaspoon fresh oregano, crumbled, *or* ½ teaspoon dried
Black pepper to taste
⅛ teaspoon no-salt seasoning
2 cups diced zucchini
3 tablespoons dry white wine
2 slices calorie-reduced whole-wheat bread, toasted
1 small tomato, sliced
2 tablespoons freshly grated Parmesan cheese
2 tablespoons grated part-skim mozzarella cheese

1. Preheat broiler.

2. Coat a medium saute pan with nonstick spray. Over low heat, saute onion and garlic with basil, oregano, pepper, and seasoning until onion is translucent. Add zucchini and saute until cooked through, 6 to 8 minutes. Splash white wine over zucchini and cook, stirring, until skillet is almost dry.

3. Divide vegetables between the two slices of toast. Arrange tomato slices over vegetables.

4. Combine the 2 cheeses in a small bowl and sprinkle over sandwiches. Broil until cheese is bubbly.

Nutritional Data

PER SERVING		EXCHANGES	
Calories:	149	Milk:	0.0
% Calories from fat:	18	Vegetable:	1.4
Fat (gm):	3.1	Fruit:	0.0
Sat. fat (gm):	1.6	Bread:	0.7
Cholesterol (mg):	6.5	Meat:	0.6
Sodium (mg):	252	Fat:	0.2
Protein (gm):	9.3		
Carbohydrate (gm):	20		

CHILI TOAST

Serves 1

1 slice calorie-reduced whole-wheat bread,
   lightly toasted
½ cup canned chicken chili

1. Spread chili on toast and microwave in a microwave-safe bowl 45 seconds (high) or until hot and bubbly, stirring once.

2. Garnish with up to 1 cup (total) of the following condiments: roasted, chopped green chili; finely chopped onion; chopped green onion; chopped tomato; salsa; shredded lettuce.

Nutritional Data

PER SERVING		EXCHANGES	
Calories:	132	Milk:	0.0
% Calories from fat:	12	Vegetable:	0.1
Fat (gm):	1.8	Fruit:	0.0
Sat. fat (gm):	0.5	Bread:	1.2
Cholesterol (mg):	22	Meat:	1.5
Sodium (mg):	538	Fat:	0.1
Protein (gm):	11.7		
Carbohydrate (gm):	18.5		

MEXICAN BLACK BEAN PIZZA

Reserve some of this topping for the next morning. Spread it over hot tortillas or toast, and cover all with a basted egg.

Serves 6

1 15-oz. can black beans, drained and rinsed
1 10-oz. pkg. frozen corn, thawed
1 tablespoon finely chopped jalapeño peppers
2 tablespoons chopped cilantro
1 tablespoon chili powder
  Garlic powder
  Vegetable cooking spray
6 whole-wheat tortillas (6 in.)
2 ozs. part-skim mozzarella cheese, shredded
1 large tomato, cut into thin wedges, *or* 1 cup
  salsa
  Nonfat sour cream, optional
2 green onions, sliced

1. Preheat oven to 375 degrees.
2. Combine black beans, corn, jalapeños, cilantro, chili powder, and garlic powder in a 2-quart saucepan set over medium heat. Cook and stir until heated through.
3. Coat 2, 9 x 12-in. baking pans with nonstick spray. Place tortillas side by side on pan. Spoon 1/3 cup of black bean mixture onto each tortilla. Sprinkle with 2 teaspoons of cheese.
4. Bake 25 minutes or until hot. Cut pizzas into wedges; garnish with tomato (or salsa), sour cream, and sliced green onions.

Nutritional Data

PER SERVING		EXCHANGES	
Calories:	248	Milk:	0.0
% Calories from fat:	13	Vegetable:	0.1
Fat (gm):	3.9	Fruit:	0.0
Sat. fat (gm):	0.9	Bread:	2.9
Cholesterol (mg):	2.7	Meat:	0.5
Sodium (mg):	196	Fat:	0.5
Protein (gm):	12.3		
Carbohydrate (gm):	44.3		

LOBSTER PUFF

Any cooked white fish, crab, or scallops may be substituted for the lobster.

Serves 2

2 tablespoons low-calorie mayonnaise
2 tablespoons finely chopped green onion
1 teaspoon Dijon-style mustard
8 ozs. cooked lobster, flaked (about 1½ cups)
2 egg whites
2 slices calorie-reduced French bread

1. Preheat broiler.

2. In a medium bowl, combine mayonnaise, chopped green onions, and mustard; stir in flaked lobster.

3. In a clean, deep glass or metal bowl, beat egg whites until stiff. Fold into lobster mixture.

4. Spoon half of mixture over each slice of bread and transfer to broiler pan. Broil until puffy, 2 to 3 minutes.

Nutritional Data

PER SERVING		EXCHANGES	
Calories:	201	Milk:	0.0
% Calories from fat:	16	Vegetable:	0.0
Fat (gm):	3.5	Fruit:	0.0
Sat. fat (gm):	0.6	Bread:	0.7
Cholesterol (mg):	83	Meat:	3.3
Sodium (mg):	596	Fat:	0.5
Protein (gm):	29		
Carbohydrate (gm):	14.3		

HALIBUT PESTO PITA

Serves 2

- 6 ozs. cook halibut, flaked
- 1/4 cup pesto (see Eggplant Pesto Sandwich, p. 80)
- 1/2 cup plain nonfat yogurt, *or* nonfat sour cream
- 1 teaspoon freshly grated lemon peel
  Tabasco sauce, to taste
- 1 whole-wheat pita, split
- 2/3 cup alfalfa sprouts
  Cherry tomatoes, for garnish
  Ripe olives, sliced, for garnish

1. Combine flaked fish, pesto, nonfat yogurt, lemon peel, and Tabasco sauce in a bowl. Taste and correct seasoning.

2. Lightly toast pita, if desired. Spread half the filling over each pita half. Arrange alfalfa sprouts over filling.

3. Garnish with sliced cherry tomatoes, or tomato roses, and sliced black olives.

Nutritional Data

PER SERVING		EXCHANGES	
Calories:	234	Milk:	0.4
% Calories from fat:	11	Vegetable:	0.1
Fat (gm):	2.9	Fruit:	0.0
Sat. fat (gm):	0.4	Bread:	1.1
Cholesterol (mg):	36	Meat:	3.1
Sodium (mg):	260	Fat:	0.1
Protein (gm):	29.1		
Carbohydrate (gm):	21.6		

SALAD PIZZA

Each day Americans eat enough pizza to cover 100 acres! This one is absolutely guilt-free—nice and light on a hot summer day.

Serves 3

1 cup nonfat cottage cheese
2 tablespoons nonfat milk
2 teaspoons Dijon-style mustard
1/4 teaspoon dill weed
1/8 teaspoon each: onion powder and
    garlic powder
3 whole-wheat tortillas (8 in.)
3 cups torn mixed greens
6 cherry tomatoes, halved
1 green onion, chopped
3 tablespoons Parmesan cheese
    Salt-free herbal mix (your favorite), to taste
    Black pepper, to taste

1. Combine cottage cheese, nonfat milk, mustard, dill weed, onion powder, and garlic powder.

2. Wrap each tortilla (flat) in a paper towel and microwave (high) 1 minute or until crisp.

3. Spread 1/3 or the cottage cheese filling over each tortilla and, on a microwave-safe dinner plate, microwave (high) 40 seconds or just until warmed.

4. Sprinkle 1/3 of the salad greens over each tortilla. Scatter tomatoes and chopped onions over greens; sprinkle with 1 tablespoon Parmesan cheese; season to taste with herbal mix and black pepper.

Nutritional Data

PER SERVING		EXCHANGES	
Calories:	205	Milk:	0.0
% Calories from fat:	19	Vegetable:	0.3
Fat (gm):	4	Fruit:	0.0
Sat. fat (gm):	1	Bread:	1.3
Cholesterol (mg):	7	Meat:	1.7
Sodium (mg):	595	Fat:	0.6
Protein (gm):	16.4		
Carbohydrate (gm):	27.7		

SUMMER VEGETABLE TOSTADA

Build this tostada as high as you like—it won't fill you up or out.
Pretty to look at, too.

Serves 1

1 corn tortilla
1 cup Marinated Vegetables, drained (recipe
   follows)
   Salsa, to taste
   Shredded iceberg lettuce, for garnish

1. Crisp corn tortilla by one of the following methods: place tortilla between two paper towels and microwave (high) 1 minute or until crisp; place tortilla on cookie sheet and bake in preheated 400-degree oven about 5 minutes.

2. Assemble tostadas by layering marinated vegetables, shredded lettuce, and salsa.

Marinated Vegetables, or "Summer in a Jar"
Makes 8 1/2-cup servings

1 gal. glass bowl or jar
8 cups assorted fresh vegetables, washed,
   trimmed, and sliced (choose among crookneck
   squash, zucchini, carrots, cauliflower, broccoli,
   green beans, pea pods, and pearl onions)
3 garlic cloves, pressed
1/2 cup chopped parsley
4 teaspoons fresh tarragon, *or* 2 teaspoons dried
1/4 cup walnut oil
1/3 cup frozen apple juice concentrate, thawed
1 cup wine vinegar
2 cups low-sodium chicken broth
2 tablespoons sugar

1. Place a steamer basket in a 2-quart saucepan. Add enough water to cover bottom of pan. Cover and bring to a boil. Lower heat and steam vegetables, by species, until just tender, 4 to 5 minutes: be careful not

to overcook! Drain. Layer vegetables in a glass bowl or jar. Add pressed garlic, parsley, and tarragon.

2. In a medium saucepan, combine walnut oil, apple juice concentrate, vinegar, broth, and sugar. Bring to a boil and pour over vegetables. Refrigerate overnight for vegetables to absorb flavors. Vegetables will last up to 10 days in refrigerator.

Nutritional Data

PER SERVING		EXCHANGES	
Calories:	231	Milk:	0.0
% Calories from fat:	27	Vegetable:	2.4
Fat (gm):	7	Fruit:	0.4
Sat. fat (gm):	0.4	Bread:	0.8
Cholesterol (mg):	0.4	Meat:	0.4
Sodium (mg):	222	Fat:	1.4
Protein (gm):	4.1		
Carbohydrate (gm):	24.9		

HOT CHEESE BAVARIAN

A little German mustard would set this Bavarian off to perfection!

Serves 1

- 1 slice rye bread, toasted
- ½ tablespoon diet margarine
- ¼ cup sauerkraut, well rinsed and drained
- ½ medium tomato, sliced
- 2 ozs. part-skim mozzarella cheese, grated

1. Preheat broiler.
2. Spread toasted bread with margarine. Cover sauerkraut and generously layer the tomato slices; sprinkle with cheese.
3. Broil until golden and bubbly. Serve steaming hot.

Nutritional Data

PER SERVING		EXCHANGES	
Calories:	243	Milk:	0.0
% Calories from fat:	29	Vegetable:	0.4
Fat (gm):	8	Fruit:	0.0
Sat. fat (gm):	3	Bread:	1.0
Cholesterol (mg):	16	Meat:	2.8
Sodium (mg):	578	Fat:	0.7
Protein (gm):	24		
Carbohydrate (gm):	20		

REUBEN PIZZA

Serves 2

1 whole-wheat tortilla (8 in.)
2 teaspoons low-sodium mustard
1 oz. low-sodium, low-fat Swiss cheese, shredded
1/3 cup sauerkraut, well rinsed and drained
1 oz. lean corned beef, shaved
1/2 teaspoon caraway seeds

1. Crisp tortilla in microwave by placing between 2 paper towels and microwave (high) until crisp, about 1 minute.

2. Spread mustard over tortilla. Sprinkle with shredded cheese, sauerkraut, corned beef, and caraway seeds. Microwave (high) until cheese melts, 1 to 1½ minutes.

Nutritional Data

PER SERVING		EXCHANGES	
Calories:	164	Milk:	0.0
% Calories from fat:	27	Vegetable:	0.4
Fat (gm):	4.8	Fruit:	0.0
Sat. fat (gm):	1.8	Bread:	0.9
Cholesterol (mg):	15	Meat:	1.2
Sodium (mg):	470	Fat:	0.4
Protein (gm):	12.6		
Carbohydrate (gm):	17		

CHEESE CRISP WITH SUN-DRIED TOMATOES & CHILIES

"Cheese crisp" is another name for a quesadilla.

Serves 2

Vegetable cooking spray
2 whole-wheat flour tortillas (8 in.)
1 cup (3 ozs.) nonfat mozzarella cheese, shredded
1 4-oz. can whole roasted chilies
1/2 cup sun-dried tomatoes
1 tablespoon chopped cilantro
Nonfat sour cream, to taste
Salsa, to taste

1. Preheat oven to 450 degrees.

2. Coat baking sheet with nonstick spray and place tortillas on sheet. Divide cheese between tortillas, sprinkling evenly. Rinse chilies, then cut into 1/4-in. strips and place on tortillas in a pinwheel design, if desired. Arrange dried tomatoes over all and sprinkle with cilantro.

3. Bake until cheese melts, about 5 minutes. Garnish with salsa and sour cream. Cut into wedges and serve immediately.

Nutritional Data

PER SERVING		EXCHANGES	
Calories:	199	Milk:	0.2
% Calories from fat:	12	Vegetable:	0.9
Fat (gm):	2.6	Fruit:	0.0
Sat. fat (gm):	0.4	Bread:	1.3
Cholesterol (mg):	8	Meat:	2.0
Sodium (mg):	478	Fat:	0.5
Protein (gm):	18		
Carbohydrate (gm):	23.3		

SHRIMP AND ASPARAGUS PIZZA

Several breads can be used as a base for quick pizzas: English muffins, corn tortillas, pita bread, Boboli, ready-to-bake pizza dough, even rice cakes! But whole-wheat tortillas are my favorite. They have more flavor, fiber, and are convenient and easy to use. For a more solid crust, crisp the tortilla (see below) before making the following pizza.

Serves 1

1 whole-wheat flour tortilla (6 in.)
1/4 cup tomato sauce
1 1/2 teaspoons prepared horseradish
1/2 teaspoon fresh dill weed, *or* 1/4 teaspoon dried
1/4 teaspoon garlic powder
2 ozs. baby shrimp, cooked and peeled
3 tablespoons asparagus tips, cooked
1/3 cup (1 oz.) shredded part-skim mozzarella cheese

1. Crisp tortilla according to directions below.
2. If using a microwave, set tortilla on a dinner plate. If using the oven, place tortilla on a baking sheet. In a small bowl, combine tomato sauce and horseradish. Spread tortilla with sauce; sprinkle with dill weed and garlic powder. Evenly cover tortilla with shrimp, asparagus tips, and shredded cheese. Either broil or microwave just until cheese melts.

Crisping methods:

Microwave: Wrap tortilla loosely in paper towels. Microwave (high) 1 to 2 minutes or until crisp.

Broiler: Arrange a double layer of aluminum foil on a broiler pan. Place 2 tortillas on broiler pan and set 3 to 4 inches from source of heat. Turn on broiler; do not preheat. Heat tortillas until a few brown spots develop and tortillas begin to crisp. Turn and brown the other side, watching carefully.

Gas Range: Flour tortillas may also be crisped over a gas flame by placing tortillas in a skillet over a low flame. Turn when brown spots appear and cook other side.

Nutritional Data

PER SERVING		EXCHANGES	
Calories:	250	Milk:	0.0
% Calories from fat:	20	Vegetable:	1.2
Fat (gm):	6	Fruit:	0.0
Sat. fat (gm):	2	Bread:	1.3
Cholesterol (mg):	35	Meat:	3.1
Sodium (mg):	598	Fat:	0.5
Protein (gm):	5.4		
Carbohydrate (gm):	25.1		

BASQUADILLAS

A Basque quesadilla! Round crackerbread or lavosh may be substituted for the tortillas.

Serves 4

3 large bell peppers: green, red, and yellow, purple, or any combination
2 teaspoons olive oil
2 tablespoons balsamic vinegar
½ teaspoon dried, crushed rosemary, *or* 1 teaspoon fresh thyme
¼ teaspoon garlic powder
2 teaspoons fresh chopped basil, *or* ¾ teaspoon dried basil
2 whole-wheat tortillas (12 in.)
3 ozs. soft goat's cheese
Basil sprigs, for garnish

1. Under broiler or on barbecue grill, roast peppers until skin blackens on all sides and bottoms are blackened or visibly pulling away from flesh. As peppers are done, remove from broiler and put in heavy plastic food bag. Let cool 10 minutes.

2. Using fingers and no running water, slip thin layer of charred skin from peppers. Remove tops and cores from peppers and cut peppers into thick strips. Remove most seeds and veins. Combine all peppers in bowl and set aside.

3. Combine olive oil, vinegar, rosemary, garlic powder, and basil in a medium bowl. Add peppers to mixture and marinate 30 minutes to 1 hour.

4. Set tortillas in a pan 3 to 4 inches under broiler. Turn on broiler. Heat tortillas until they turn a light brown and begin to crisp. Turn and brown the second side, watching carefully not to burn.

5. Spread half the goat's cheese over each tortilla. Drain vegetables and divide between tortillas. Cut each Basquadilla into 6 slices. Garnish with fresh basil sprigs.

Cook's Note: Microwaving is fast, but for a deeper flavor, roast peppers in the oven. Simply line a cookie sheet with foil, set oven at 450 degrees, and roast 10 to 15 minutes or until tender.

Nutritional Data

PER SERVING		EXCHANGES	
Calories:	245	Milk:	0.0
% Calories from fat:	29	Vegetable:	2.2
Fat (gm):	8	Fruit:	0.0
Sat. fat (gm):	2.3	Bread:	1.0
Cholesterol (mg):	12	Meat:	0.4
Sodium (mg):	212	Fat:	1.4
Protein (gm):	9.4		
Carbohydrate (gm):	36.3		

SUMMER GARDEN SANDWICH

Well worth the time to assemble—delicious!

Serves 4

1 10-oz. pkg. frozen chopped spinach, thawed
1/2 cup chopped onions
1/2 cup chopped green onions, including tops
1/2 cup chopped green bell pepper
1 medium tomato, chopped
3 tablespoons nonfat sour cream
2 tablespoons low-calorie mayonnaise
2 teaspoons Dijon-style mustard

Dash Tabasco
Herbal seasoning, to taste
1 cup grated part-skim mozzarella cheese
½ cup grated reduced-calorie Cheddar cheese
8 slices reduced-calorie whole-wheat bread
4 large tomato slices
Alfalfa sprouts, for garnish

1. Preheat broiler.
2. In a medium bowl, combine spinach, both onions, green peppers, and tomatoes. In another smaller bowl, combine sour cream, mayonnaise, mustard, Tabasco, and herbal seasoning, and mix well. Stir mayonnaise mixture into the vegetables.
3. Combine grated cheeses in a bowl and toss to mix.
4. Spread spinach mixture evenly over 4 slices of bread, and top each with a tomato slice. Spread cheese mixture evenly over other bread slices.
5. Broil spinach slices until bread is lightly browned. Broil cheese slices until cheese melts. Garnish all slices with sprouts. Serve spinach and cheese slices, side by side, open face.

Nutritional Data

PER SERVING		EXCHANGES	
Calories:	223	Milk:	0.0
% Calories from fat:	22	Vegetable:	1.1
Fat (gm):	5.9	Fruit:	0.0
Sat. fat (gm):	2.6	Bread:	1.4
Cholesterol (mg):	14	Meat:	1.5
Sodium (mg):	577	Fat:	0.5
Protein (gm):	18.6		
Carbohydrate (gm):	30		

QUESADILLAS WITH PEACH SALSA

Serves 4

1 15-oz. can peaches in juice, drained, finely diced
¼ cup sliced green onions
1 tablespoon lemon juice
1 bell pepper, any color, finely diced
1 4-oz. can green chilies, diced
¼ teaspoon ground ginger
4 whole-wheat flour tortillas (6 in.)
4 ozs. (1⅓ cups) part-skim mozzarella cheese, shredded

1. Make salsa: Combine first 6 ingredients and mix well; set aside.

2. Place 1 tortilla on a dinner plate. Sprinkle ⅓ cup cheese evenly over tortilla. Spoon peach salsa over cheese. Microwave (high) 10 minutes or until cheese melts. Repeat with other tortillas. Refrigerate any remaining salsa.

Nutritional Data

PER SERVING		EXCHANGES	
Calories:	248	Milk:	0.1
% Calories from fat:	16	Vegetable:	0.6
Fat (gm):	4.1	Fruit:	0.5
Sat. fat (gm):	1.5	Bread:	1.3
Cholesterol (mg):	13	Meat:	2.7
Sodium (mg):	547	Fat:	0.5
Protein (gm):	21.1		
Carbohydrate (gm):	30.7		

PIÑA COLADA SHORTCAKE

Serves 4

  2 English muffins, split
1⅓ cups nonfat cottage cheese
  ¼ cup pineapple chunks in juice, drained
  2 tablespoons unsweetened coconut
  ½ teaspoon rum, *or* ¼ teaspoon rum extract
  2 ozs. extra-lean boiled ham, chopped

1. Preheat broiler.
2. Toast split English muffins under broiler until lightly brown.
3. Combine cottage cheese, pineapple, coconut, and rum, mixing well. Stir in ham.
4. Divide mixture in fourths and spread over muffin halves. Broil until warmed, 1 to 2 minutes.

Nutritional Data

PER SERVING		EXCHANGES	
Calories:	153	Milk:	0.0
% Calories from fat:	11	Vegetable:	0.0
Fat (gm):	1.9	Fruit:	0.2
Sat. fat (gm):	0.8	Bread:	0.8
Cholesterol (mg):	10	Meat:	1.8
Sodium (mg):	464	Fat:	0.4
Protein (gm):	14.8		
Carbohydrate (gm):	19.4		

LAVOSH HEARTS WITH SPINACH PESTO

Sourdough baguettes would be wonderful in place of lavosh. Do remember the chilled wine, Greek olives, and bunches of grapes if you have a picnic. The Spinach Pesto can also be mixed into cooked pasta or spooned over poached fish and broiled chicken.

Serves 4 (2 hearts each)

- 1/4 cup Spinach Pesto (recipe follows)
- 1 anchovy, minced, *or* 2 teaspoons anchovy paste
- 8 heart-shaped lavosh crackers
- 1/2 cup lowfat ricotta cheese
- 1 large tomato, chopped finely
- 2 tablespoons freshly grated Parmesan cheese

1. In a small bowl, combine pesto with anchovy until well blended. Spread ricotta cheese over crackers, followed by 1 tablespoon pesto. Sprinkle with chopped tomato and Parmesan cheese.

Spinach Pesto
Makes 1/4 cup

- 1/3 cup fresh parsley
- 1 garlic clove
- 1 1/4 cups fresh spinach leaves, loosely packed
- 1 tablespoon freshly grated Parmesan cheese
- 2 teaspoons olive oil
- 2 teaspoons lemon juice
- 1 teaspoon seasoned rice vinegar

1. Position knife blade in food processor bowl; top with cover. Drop parsley and garlic clove through food chute with processor running; process 15 seconds or until minced.

2. Add spinach and remaining ingredients; process 30 seconds. Scrape bowl with a rubber spatula, and process an additional 30 seconds or until smooth.

Nutritional Data *(includes 1 tablespoon pesto)*

PER SERVING		EXCHANGES	
Calories:	115	Milk:	0.2
% Calories from fat:	27	Vegetable:	0.1
Fat (gm):	1.2	Fruit:	0.0
Sat. fat (gm):	1.1	Bread:	0.6
Cholesterol (mg):	7.5	Meat:	0.6
Sodium (mg):	201	Fat:	0.1
Protein (gm):	7		
Carbohydrate (gm):	11.8		

COUNTRY FRENCH TUNA PÂTÉ ON SOURDOUGH TOAST

Canned tuna can be elegant, rich, and souffle-like when combined with light sour cream and suspended in gelatin. Besides being attractive, you'll have a powerhouse of lean protein. Serve in stoneware crocks or mold in small, decorative molds.

Serves 6

¼ cup water

1 envelope plain gelatin

1 6½-oz. can tuna in water, drained

1 cup plain nonfat sour cream

¾ cup fruity white wine, such as Chenin Blanc

¼ cup minced scallions

¾ teaspoon dried, *or* 1 tablespoon fresh, tarragon

1 tablespoon chopped fresh parsley

6 slices calorie-reduced sourdough bread

1½ tablespoons olive oil

Nonfat sour cream, capers, minced green onions, chopped egg white, sliced almonds, chopped parsley, and fresh tarragon, optional for garnish

1. Pour water into a small saucepan and sprinkle gelatin over surface. Allow gelatin to rest 1 minute; heat water to barely a simmer.

2. Pour gelatin mixture into blender with tuna, sour cream, and wine. Process until smooth. Pour into a bowl and stir in scallions, tarragon, and parsley. Chill 3 to 4 hours or until firm.

3. Using a pastry brush, stroke olive oil over each slice of bread. Toast under broiler until lightly crisp, 3 to 4 minutes. (Watch carefully so toast doesn't burn!)

4. Spread about ¹/₃ cup of pâté over each slice of warm toast. Garnish with any of the ingredients listed.

Nutritional Data

PER SERVING		EXCHANGES	
Calories:	163	Milk:	0.3
% Calories from fat:	23	Vegetable:	0.0
Fat (gm):	4.2	Fruit:	0.0
Sat. fat (gm):	0.6	Bread:	0.7
Cholesterol (mg):	9	Meat:	1.1
Sodium (mg):	239	Fat:	0.8
Protein (gm):	13.7		
Carbohydrate (gm):	14.3		

BEER CHEESE PUFF

Serves 2

Vegetable cooking spray
2 slices pumpernickel bread
³/₄ cup nonfat cottage cheese
2 ozs. (about ¹/₂ cup) low-sodium, low-fat Cheddar cheese, shredded
1 tablespoon Parmesan cheese
¹/₄ cup light beer, or non-alcoholic beer
¹/₃ cup minced scallion
Dash Worcestershire sauce
Dash hot pepper sauce, such as Tabasco

1. Preheat broiler.

2. Coat a 9 x 12-in. baking sheet with nonstick spray and place bread under broiler until lightly toasted on both sides, 2 to 3 minutes. (Watch carefully so toast doesn't burn!)

3. In a small bowl, combine all 3 cheeses, beer, scallions, Worcestershire sauce, and hot pepper sauce. Spread half of mixture over each slice of pumpernickel. Broil 3 to 4 minutes or until bubbly.

Nutritional Data

PER SERVING		EXCHANGES	
Calories:	195	Milk:	0.0
% Calories from fat:	20	Vegetable:	0.0
Fat (gm):	4.4	Fruit:	0.0
Sat. fat (gm):	2	Bread:	1.0
Cholesterol (mg):	16	Meat:	2.4
Sodium (mg):	570	Fat:	0.4
Protein (gm):	19.4		
Carbohydrate (gm):	18.6		

3.
POWER LUNCH
FAVORITES

A "Power Lunch" fuels both the body and the mind. Power foods are primarily protein and complex carbohydrates. Research indicates that chemicals released from amino acids, the building blocks of protein, tend to maintain mental sharpness and an alert, focused mind. Excess fat, on the other hand, slows digestion and diverts blood from the brain to the intestinal tract, resulting in sluggishness, unclear thinking, and increased likelihood of weight gain. Fat has 9 calories per gram compared to 4 calories for both protein and carbohydrate.

Permanent weight loss actually happens from the *inside,* **out.** After we consult our feelings and determine that we are or *are not* hungry, making the best food choices is the next step. Knowing the fat content of foods is the single most important factor in choosing wisely. When we know that fat, though invisible, is still there, hidden within salad dressings, whole milk cheeses, and rich-tasting breads such as croissants, we may well choose alternatives—and eventually we may prefer these alternatives!

A delicatessen tuna salad sandwich and one homemade will serve as an example of the nutritional value of choosing foods wisely:

Deli Sandwich	Calories	Fat, grams
Tuna packed in oil, 3 ounces	169	24.8
Mayonnaise, 2 tablespoons	200	11.2
Almonds or walnuts, 1 tablespoon	44	3.7
Avocado half, sliced	153	15.0
Alfalfa sprouts, ½ cup	20	.3
Hearty deli bread, 2 slices	160	2.0
	746	**57**

Sandwich from Home		
Tuna packed in water, 3 ounces	111	0
Nonfat mayonnaise, 1 tablespoon	12	0
Celery, chopped, ¼ cup	10	0
Tomato slices and alfalfa sprouts	35	0
Calorie-reduced whole-wheat bread, 2 slices	80	0
	248	**0**

What you might think of as a low-fat tuna salad sandwich may well be laden with fat. The deli tuna sandwich example above derives 47 percent of it calories from fat! Hearty, high-fat sandwiches are a fortifying lunch for the physically active such as lumberjacks, construction workers, and those who have a high metabolism. For most of us, however, this is not reality. One gram of fat contains more than twice the calories of protein or carbohydrate and thus is more likely to add up to excess weight. Also never assume that low cholesterol means low fat. A food advertised as low cholesterol may still be high in fat and therefore high in calories.

Freezer Sandwiches

An especially clever timesaving idea is to make a batch of sandwiches and freeze them for the whole week. Wrap sandwiches separately in plastic bags or waxed paper. Place all the sandwiches of one kind in a large container or plastic bag, securely tightly, and label the contents. This allows you or members of your family to take the sandwich of their choice for their own lunches. Throw a frozen sandwich in the lunchbox early in the morning, and, presto, it's thawed in 3 to 4 hours, just in time for lunch.

To prepare a sandwich for freezing, spread a light coating of diet margarine on both slices of bread. Other spreads that freeze well are mustard, ketchup, relishes and chutneys, chili sauce, and peanut butter. Cooked meats and hard cheese may be frozen. Although the cheese may become crumbly, the taste is the same.

Do not use mayonnaise, salad dressing, yogurt, sour cream, cottage cheese, or cream cheese in frozen sandwiches, as they will separate or change their textures. Do not freeze egg whites, fruits such as oranges and kiwi, vegetables including lettuce and tomatoes, and very moist fillings. Sandwiches may be frozen up to one week.

"BEEFSTEAK" SANDWICH

Buying your produce at the farmers' market has nutritious benefits. Vine-ripened tomatoes contain, ounce for ounce, more than 2½ times the beta carotene and twice as much vitamin C as artificially ripened store-bought tomatoes, according to "Eating Well" magazine. This recipe has been modified from an old Pennsylvania Dutch recipe for fried red tomatoes although green tomatoes may be substituted.

Serves 1

1 tablespoon whole-wheat flour
2 teaspoons brown sugar
½ vine-ripened Beefsteak tomato, sliced
  ¼-in. thick
  Butter-flavored vegetable cooking spray
2 slices calorie-reduced rye *or* whole-wheat, bread
1 tablespoon Dijon-style mustard
4 tablespoons nonfat sour cream
  Salt and freshly ground black pepper, to taste

1. Combine flour and brown sugar in a plastic bag and shake. Drop sliced tomatoes in bag and shake again to coat.

2. Coat a nonstick 8-in. skillet with butter-flavored vegetable spray, and heat skillet over low-medium heat. Saute tomatoes until lightly crisp, 4 to 5 minutes, turning a few times. Use nonstick spray after turning each time to keep the coating crunchy. Remove from heat.

3. Spread one slice of bread with mustard, then cover both slices with sour cream. Add tomato slices and season with salt and pepper. Press bread slices together and enjoy a nutritious indulgence!

Nutritional Data

PER SERVING		EXCHANGES	
Calories:	214	Milk:	0.2
% Calories from fat:	9	Vegetable:	0.3
Fat (gm):	2.3	Fruit:	0.0
Sat. fat (gm):	0.2	Bread:	2.4
Cholesterol (mg):	0	Meat:	0.0
Sodium (mg):	598	Fat:	0.2
Protein (gm):	8.9		
Carbohydrate (gm):	42.3		

TABBOULEH BUNDLES

Romaine leaves encase a light, delicious filling—sort of a summer burrito. If made ahead, you may refrigerate until the next day. Bundles hold up for as long as 5 hours at room temperature.

Serves 2 (2 rolls each)

- ½ cup bulgur
- 1 large tomato, chopped
- 4 ozs. frozen cooked shrimp, thawed
- ¼ cup chopped scallions
- 1 cup chopped fresh flat-leaf parsley
- 2 tablespoons crushed dried mint
- ¼ cup chopped onion
- ¼ teaspoon black pepper
- 1 cup lowfat plain yogurt
- 8 large romaine leaves

1. Cover bulgur with hot water and let it stand 30 minutes. Drain bulgur in colander.

2. In a large bowl, combine bulgur, chopped tomato, shrimp, scallions, parsley, mint, and onions. Mix well. Add pepper and yogurt. Stir mixture until well blended.

3. In a 10 or 12-in. saucepan, bring about 1 in. of water to a boil. Immerse romaine leaves one at a time, just until limp, about 5 seconds. Immediately immerse leaves in ice water until cold. Lift out and lay leaves flat on paper towels; blot dry.

4. At stem end of each leaf, mound ¼ cup of filling. Fold sides over filling, then roll from stem end, tucking in edges as you go, to form a neat package. Serve, or seal in plastic wrap to store or carry.

Nutritional Data

PER SERVING		EXCHANGES	
Calories:	136	Milk:	0.2
% Calories from fat:	7	Vegetable:	0.1
Fat (gm):	1	Fruit:	0.0
Sat. fat (gm):	0.1	Bread:	0.5
Cholesterol (mg):	7.4	Meat:	0.4
Sodium (mg):	216	Fat:	
Protein (gm):	12.1		
Carbohydrate (gm):	20.6		

BARBECUED TUNA BUNS

"Barbecues," or "Sloppy Joes," never go out of style. This one's fat free.

Serves 2

1 6½-oz. can water-packed tuna, rinsed and
  drained
½ cup finely chopped celery
¼ cup finely chopped onion
2 tablespoons brown sugar
2 teaspoons low-sodium mustard
1 tablespoon red wine vinegar
1 cup low-sodium tomato juice
2 calorie-reduced hamburger buns, toasted

1. Combine all ingredients, except buns, in a 2-quart saucepan. Simmer, covered, 20 to 30 minutes.

2. Spoon barbecue over toasted hamburger buns.

Nutritional Data

PER SERVING		EXCHANGES	
Calories:	227	Milk:	0.0
% Calories from fat:	9	Vegetable:	0.8
Fat (gm):	2.1	Fruit:	0.0
Sat. fat (gm):	0.1	Bread:	1.5
Cholesterol (mg):	18.7	Meat:	2.2
Sodium (mg):	446	Fat:	0.2
Protein (gm):	21.4		
Carbohydrate (gm):	31		

SMOKIN' CHILI SANDWICH

Chilies tend to raise metabolic levels, and therefore our bodies burn more calories simply by eating them! For chili lovers, this sandwich may be the ideal breakfast or lunch.

Serves 2

- 4 medium Anaheim chilies, *or* 4-oz. can whole chilies
- 1/4 cup calorie-reduced mayonnaise
- 2–3 drops liquid smoke
- Chopped cilantro, optional
- Dash garlic powder
- Vegetable cooking spray
- 3/4 cup egg substitute
- 4 slices calorie-reduced French bread, toasted
- 1/2 medium tomato, sliced
- Salt and pepper, to taste

1. Preheat broiler. Place chilies under heat until black, 1 to 2 minutes. Turn and broil until all sides are roasted.

2. Combine mayonnaise, liquid smoke, cilantro, and garlic powder.

3. Coat an 8-in. nonstick skillet and bring to medium heat. Beat egg substitute with 1 tablespoon of water and pour into pan, making an 8-in. round pancake. Cook until firm and flip; cook until done and remove from heat. Using a spatula, cut in half.

4. Wear rubber gloves and keep hands away from eyes and mouth while handling chilies. Cut tops off chilies and pull the seeds out. Cut open and remove remaining seeds; remove and discard skins.

5. Spread 1 tablespoon of mayonnaise mixture over one side of all 4 slices of toasted bread. Assemble each sandwich using 2 chilies, omelet (fold if necessary), and a slice or two of tomato. Season to taste with salt and pepper. Slice sandwiches into triangles.

Nutritional Data

PER SERVING		EXCHANGES	
Calories:	249	Milk:	0.0
% Calories from fat:	29	Vegetable:	2.2
Fat (gm):	8.4	Fruit:	0.0
Sat. fat (gm):	1.2	Bread:	1.4
Cholesterol (mg):	10	Meat:	1.1
Sodium (mg):	366	Fat:	1.6
Protein (gm):	13.2		
Carbohydrate (gm):	33.3		

CALICO BEAN SANDWICH

Try eating something sour the next time you crave something sweet. It may, oddly enough, satisfy your taste buds.

Serves 3

1 cup cooked beans*
2 tablespoons finely chopped onion
2 tablespoons chopped green chilies
2 tablespoons chopped dill, *or* sour, pickles
1 tablespoon prepared mustard
3 calorie-reduced whole-wheat buns
3 slices low-fat processed sharp cheese
3 thick tomato slices
   Alfalfa sprouts, for garnish

1. Preheat oven to broil.

2. In a small bowl, combine beans, onions, chilies, pickles, and mustard. Toast buns lightly under broiler.

3. Spread filling on toasted buns. Place cheese slices over filling and broil until bubbly. Arrange tomato slices and alfalfa sprouts on top. Serve filling with extra mustard and pickles and perhaps a bowl of hot, steamy soup.

*Use pinto beans, black or red beans, garbanzos, or any combination thereof.

Nutritional Data

PER SERVING		EXCHANGES	
Calories:	202	Milk:	0.1
% Calories from fat:	9	Vegetable:	0.2
Fat (gm):	2	Fruit:	0.0
Sat. fat (gm):	0.1	Bread:	1.8
Cholesterol (mg):	2.5	Meat:	0.3
Sodium (mg):	579	Fat:	0.2
Protein (gm):	14.6		
Carbohydrate (gm):	6		

FRUIT COCKTAIL POCKETS

Serves 2

1/2 cup nonfat cottage cheese
1/4 cup shredded fat-free mozzarella cheese
1 cup fruit cocktail packed in water, drained
2 tablespoons sliced almonds
    Lettuce leaves, for garnish
1 pita bread, cut in half

1. In a small bowl, combine cottage cheese, shredded cheese, fruit cocktail, and sliced almonds.

2. Open pockets and line both halves with lettuce. Spoon filling into pockets.

Note: If toting lunch away from home, pack pita bread and lettuce in separate plastic bags. Pack filling in a covered container, and remember the spoon to fill the pita on-site.

Nutritional Data

PER SERVING		EXCHANGES	
Calories:	240	Milk:	0.1
% Calories from fat:	15	Vegetable:	0.0
Fat (gm):	4.1	Fruit:	0.7
Sat. fat (gm):	0.4	Bread:	1.1
Cholesterol (mg):	7.5	Meat:	2.4
Sodium (mg):	519	Fat:	0.8
Protein (gm):	21.3		
Carbohydrate (gm):	31.2		

PEANUT BUTTER CHOW CHOW ON WHOLE-WHEAT BUNS

Fresh fruit and vegetables team with peanut butter (which is 77 percent fat; reduced-fat peanut butter is 57 percent fat) for a high-fiber/low-fat sandwich.

Serves 3

- ¼ cup apple juice
- 3 tablespoons reduced-fat crunchy peanut butter
- 3 tablespoons raisins
- ½ cup chopped apple
- 1 cup shredded cabbage
- ⅓ cup shredded carrot
- 3 calorie-reduced whole-wheat hamburger buns

1. Combine apple juice, peanut butter, raisins, and chopped apples. Stir in cabbage and shredded carrots.

2. Spread filling over bottoms of each bun. Cover with top of bun.

Nutritional Data

PER SERVING		EXCHANGES	
Calories:	250	Milk:	0.0
% Calories from fat:	25	Vegetable:	0.2
Fat (gm):	6.8	Fruit:	1.7
Sat. fat (gm):	1.2	Bread:	2.0
Cholesterol (mg):	0	Meat:	0.0
Sodium (mg):	321	Fat:	1.4
Protein (gm):	6.5		
Carbohydrate (gm):	41.5		

SWEET PEPPER AND CHEESE SANDWICH*

Skinny, buttery sandwiches are comforting. This one is nourishing and creative, too, when you try your hand at the extra skinny variation, below. For an extra-soothing lunch, enjoy with a mug of steamy hot tomato soup.

Serves 1

½ medium red bell pepper
  Butter-flavored vegetable cooking spray
2 slices extra-thin sliced white bread
2 teaspoons diet margarine
1½ ozs. nonfat sharp Cheddar cheese, sliced
  Freshly ground black pepper
  Freshly chopped parsley, optional

1. Clean, seed, and finely chop pepper. Spray nonstick skillet with vegetable spray, and saute pepper until limp and roasted, about 5 minutes. Set aside and wipe out skillet.

2. Coat skillet again with vegetable spray. Spread 1 teaspoon margarine on each slice of bread. Place one slice, buttered side down, in pan. Arrange cheese on bread with the sauteed pepper and a generous dash of black pepper. Sprinkle with parsley, if desired. Cover with other bread slice, buttered side up. Cook over medium heat until sandwich is lightly brown on one side, 1 minute or so. Turn sandwich and cook another 1 to 2 minutes.

3. Cut sandwich in half diagonally and then again, making 4 of the skinniest, most delicious sandwiches you've ever eaten!

Extra skinny variation: Cover sandwich in skillet with waxed paper. Place bottom of a slightly smaller, clean, heavy skillet directly on sandwich. If a heavy skillet is unavailable, weigh it down with a can of food.

Nutritional Data

PER SERVING		EXCHANGES	
Calories:	199	Milk:	0.2
% Calories from fat:	21	Vegetable:	0.5
Fat (gm):	5	Fruit:	0.0
Sat. fat (gm):	0.9	Bread:	1.4
Cholesterol (mg):	24.3	Meat:	2.0
Sodium (mg):	598	Fat:	0.9
Protein (gm):	18		
Carbohydrate (gm):	24.3		

SALMON PARCEL

Fish is considered "brain food" because it is high in protein and low in fat. In general, eating protein foods increases alertness and has an energizing effect on the mind. Although salmon is considered a "high-fat" fish, it is an excellent source of the heart-healthy omega 3 oils. The type of salmon determines its fat content. Note these wide differences for a three-ounce raw portion!*

Pink	*2.9 grams*
Chum	*3.2 grams*
Chinook, smoked	*3.7 grams*
Coho	*5.1 grams*
Atlantic	*5.4 grams*
Chinook	*8.9 grams*

Other excellent sources of polyunsaturated omega 3 oils are mackerel, herring, cod, sardines, rainbow trout, shrimp, oysters, halibut, tuna, sablefish, bass, flounder, and anchovies. Prepare this excellent source of protein and omega 3s in the evening before.

Serves 1

- 2 large iceberg, *or* curly, lettuce leaves
- 1 3-oz. coho salmon steak
- Juice of 1/4 lemon
- Freshly ground black pepper
- 1/2 teaspoon chopped chives
- 2 tablespoons nonfat tartar sauce
- 2 slices pumpernickel cocktail rye bread

1. Place salmon steak in one corner of a lettuce leaf. Press lemon juice over fish. Sprinkle with black pepper and chives.

2. Wrap salmon steak firmly in the lettuce leaf and then wrap again in second leaf. Microwave 2 minutes (high). Chill. Serve cold with tartar sauce and cocktail rye bread.

Nutritional Data

PER SERVING		EXCHANGES	
Calories:	247	Milk:	0.0
% Calories from fat:	24	Vegetable:	0.2
Fat (gm):	7.3	Fruit:	0.7
Sat. fat (gm):	1.5	Bread:	0.7
Cholesterol (mg):	43.8	Meat:	2.6
Sodium (mg):	585	Fat:	0.1
Protein (gm):	20.6		
Carbohydrate (gm):	21.2		

*Jean Pennington's *Food Values*, 15th edition.

TINA'S LASAGNA ROLLS

Created by my sister for a family potluck, this lasagna-like sandwich is easy to put together and very high in body-building protein.

Serves 12

6 ozs. (about 1⅓ cups) cooked crab, *or* imitation crabmeat
2 cups 1% low-fat cottage cheese
¼ cup Parmesan cheese
¼ teaspoon garlic powder
3 tablespoons chopped fresh parsley
1 teaspoon dried, crushed oregano
¼ teaspoon dried, crushed marjoram
2 teaspoons dried, crushed basil
12 1-oz. dinner rolls, hollowed out to ½-in shells
1½ cups tomato sauce

1. Combine crab, cottage cheese, Parmesan cheese, garlic powder, and spices in a medium bowl.

2. Hollow out rolls and fill each with ¼ cup of filling. Spoon 2 tablespoons of tomato sauce over each roll.

3. Serve cold or warm. To serve warm, microwave (medium) 1 to 2 minutes or until warmed through.

Nutritional Data

PER SERVING		EXCHANGES	
Calories:	115	Milk:	0.0
% Calories from fat:	20	Vegetable:	0.4
Fat (gm):	2.5	Fruit:	0.0
Sat. fat (gm):	0.9	Bread:	0.6
Cholesterol (mg):	13.8	Meat:	1.0
Sodium (mg):	567	Fat:	0.3
Protein (gm):	9.1		
Carbohydrate (gm):	13.9		

TUNA HAWAIIAN

Tuna can be prepared in myriad ways and need never be boring! Try this surprisingly delicious flavor combination.

Serves 3

1 6½-oz. can tuna in water, rinsed and drained
4 ozs. nonfat sour cream
½ cup crushed pineapple in juice, drained
½ teaspoon rum extract
½ cup minced green, *or* purple, bell pepper
4 tablespoons unsweetened coconut, flaked
1 teaspoon sugar
6 slices calorie-reduced oat bran bread
3 curly lettuce leaves
Pansy, for garnish

1. Combine tuna, sour cream, pineapple, rum extract, minced pepper, coconut, and sugar in a mixing bowl. Stir until well blended.

2. Divide filling among 3 slices of bread. Spread filling over bread and top with lettuce leaves. Cover with top slices and cut sandwiches in half.

3. Garnish with an edible flower, such as a rose, pansy, or carnation, or cut-out a flower design from a yellow or green bell pepper.

Nutritional Data

PER SERVING		EXCHANGES	
Calories:	249	Milk:	0.3
% Calories from fat:	14	Vegetable:	0.5
Fat (gm):	3.9	Fruit:	0.4
Sat. fat (gm):	2.8	Bread:	1.4
Cholesterol (mg):	18	Meat:	2.2
Sodium (mg):	463	Fat:	0.7
Protein (gm):	21.1		
Carbohydrate (gm):	35		

SOURDOUGH CLAM BUNDLES

Serves 4

4 round, crispy sourdough rolls
1 tablespoon diet margarine, melted
1 10-oz. can clams, drained
2 egg whites, beaten
1 tablespoon nonfat milk
1 teaspoon fresh-snipped basil, *or* ¼ teaspoon dried
2 tablespoons chopped fresh parsley
Vegetable cooking spray
3 tomatoes, skinned and chopped

1. Slice a small round off the top of each roll and reserve. Scoop out the roll's inside to within ¼ in. of shell. Brush inside of rolls with melted margarine. Bake in a 350-degree oven 5 minutes.

2. Combine clams, egg whites, milk, basil, and parsley. Coat an 8 to 10-in. nonstick pan with vegetable spray and bring to medium heat. Stir in mixture. Cook gently, stirring, until egg whites become soft and creamy. Stir in tomato.

3. Pile filling into hot rolls, replace lids, and serve hot.

Nutritional Data

PER SERVING		EXCHANGES	
Calories:	115	Milk:	0.0
% Calories from fat:	22	Vegetable:	0.2
Fat (gm):	2.8	Fruit:	0.0
Sat. fat (gm):	0.5	Bread:	1.0
Cholesterol (mg):	0.2	Meat:	0.3
Sodium (mg):	399	Fat:	0.5
Protein (gm):	5.5		
Carbohydrate (gm):	16.8		

AN AUSTRALIAN CLASSIC: THE VEGEMITE SANDWICH

Put yer laughing gear 'round a Vegemite sandwich, mate. Wash her down with a tinnie of non-alcoholic beer. This is a beaut of a sandwich!

Serves 1

2 slices enriched white bread
1 tablespoon low-calorie mayonnaise
½ teaspoon Vegemite* yeast extract
1 ¾-oz. slice low-fat, low-sodium Cheddar cheese
Thin slices of tomato, optional
Curly lettuce leaf, for garnish
Thin slices of cucumber, optional

1. Spread mayonnaise over one side of both slices of bread.
2. Follow with a smear of the yeast extract. (If yeast spread is new to you, begin with just a half-teaspoon.) Layer cheese slice, tomato slices, lettuce, and cucumber, finishing with second slice of bread, mayonnaise side down. Cut in half diagonally.

Vegemite is a concentrated yeast extract indigenous to Australia. Used sparingly, yeast extract punctuates with a strong beefy taste. Very high in B complex vitamins, amino acids, and other minerals, Vegemite is composed primarily of protein without the fat for just 5 calories per half-teaspoon serving. Available in some gourmet and health food stores or by mail from Robern Australia, 351 Rancho Camino, Fallbrook, California 92028.

Nutritional Data

PER SERVING		EXCHANGES	
Calories:	250	Milk:	0.0
% Calories from fat:	29	Vegetable:	0.4
Fat (gm):	8	Fruit:	0.0
Sat. fat (gm):	3.1	Bread:	1.6
Cholesterol (mg):	16.9	Meat:	1.0
Sodium (mg):	423	Fat:	0.9
Protein (gm):	12.2		
Carbohydrate (gm):	33.1		

MONET PICNIC LOAF

You can earn the reputation of an artist with this sandwich! Colorful and impressionistic-looking, the tuna-vegetable salad is held together with gelatin and stuffed into a hollowed-out loaf of bread. Each slice is a prism of color like a Monet. Paint your own by shredding the vegetables instead of chopping them and varying the fresh herbs. Or substitute green, yellow, and/or purple peppers for the red.

Serves 12

- 1 lb. unsliced sandwich loaf of bread
- 1/2 cup orange juice
- 2 envelopes unflavored gelatin
- 2 6 1/2-oz. cans tuna, packed in water, drained, flaked
- 1 cup white wine
- 1 1/2 cups nonfat sour cream
- 1 tablespoon Dijon-style mustard
- 3 cups assorted finely chopped, *or* shredded, vegetables, such as spinach, colored bell peppers, peas, corn, red cabbage, scallions, and chilies
- 1 tablespoon fresh, *or* 1 1/2 teaspoons dried, dill weed

½ cup chopped fresh cilantro, *or* parsley
1 lime, grated rind and juice
1 lime, cut into 12 slices

1. Slice off end of sandwich loaf and reserve. Scoop out center of loaf with a fork, leaving a ¼-in. shell.

2. In a glass measuring cup, sprinkle gelatin over orange juice. Microwave (high) 15 to 30 seconds or just until juice rises up; stir and microwave a few seconds more until gelatin is dissolved.

3. Combine orange juice and gelatin mixture with tuna, wine, sour cream, mustard, vegetables, dill weed, cilantro, and lime juice and rind in a large bowl and blend thoroughly. Spoon into prepared shell and pack firmly. Wrap tightly with aluminum foil and refrigerate until chilled. Cut into slices and serve with slices of lime.

Nutritional Data

PER SERVING		EXCHANGES	
Calories:	95	Milk:	0.0
% Calories from fat:	9	Vegetable:	0.4
Fat (gm):	0.9	Fruit:	0.1
Sat. fat (gm):	0.1	Bread:	0.4
Cholesterol (mg):	9	Meat:	1.1
Sodium (mg):	211	Fat:	0.1
Protein (gm):	10.4		
Carbohydrate (gm):	8.5		

ROSY FISH ROLLS

Fish is naturally dyed a rosy pink in this recipe as it absorbs color from the purple cabbage. Beet horseradish can be found in the deli case of most supermarkets. These rolls are named after my sister Rosie.

6 large purple cabbage leaves
1 lb. light fish, such as cod, hake, orange roughy, and whiting, cooked and flaked
¼ cup nonfat mayonnaise
2 teaspoons beet horseradish

¼ teaspoon seasoning salt
⅛ teaspoon white pepper

1. Wrap cabbage leaves in microwave-safe plastic and microwave 2 minutes (high) or until soft and pliable.

2. In small bowl, combine remaining ingredients.

3. Spoon 2 tablespoons of filling on the edge of a single cabbage leaf and roll up, tucking sides in as if rolling a burrito. Warm in a microwave oven until heated through, either covered or uncovered, about 2 minutes per roll.

Nutritional Data

PER SERVING		EXCHANGES	
Calories:	80	Milk:	0.0
% Calories from fat:	7	Vegetable:	0.4
Fat (gm):	0.5	Fruit:	0.0
Sat. fat (gm):	0.1	Bread:	0.1
Cholesterol (mg):	32.9	Meat:	1.9
Sodium (mg):	190	Fat:	0.0
Protein (gm):	14		
Carbohydrate (gm):	4.3		

TURKEY SALAD BUNWICH WITH GREEN CHILI DRESSING

Serves 8

1 cup nonfat sour cream
4 ozs. green chilies, chopped
2 tablespoons finely chopped onion
1 tablespoon chopped cilantro
2 teaspoons Dijon-style mustard
½ teaspoon garlic salt
  Coarse black pepper, to taste
4 cups diced roasted turkey breast
2 stalks celery, chopped fine
1 green apple, chopped
8 calorie-reduced whole-wheat hamburger buns

1. Combine sour cream, green chilies, onions, cilantro, mustard, garlic salt, and pepper. Chill 1 hour to blend flavors.

2. Mix in remaining ingredients, except buns. Toast buns, if desired, and fill each one. Cover with top bun, press down, and enjoy with a cup of soup or a glass of light beer.

Nutritional Data

PER SERVING		EXCHANGES	
Calories:	234	Milk:	0.2
% Calories from fat:	10	Vegetable:	0.1
Fat (gm):	2.5	Fruit:	0.9
Sat. fat (gm):	0.3	Bread:	0.9
Cholesterol (mg):	47	Meat:	2.5
Sodium (mg):	426	Fat:	0.2
Protein (gm):	23.8		
Carbohydrate (gm):	29.4		

ENSENADA CRAB ROLL

Tuck a small rose under the tie, which can be made from a green onion, a piece of ribbon, or a stem of cilantro.

Serves 1

1 whole-wheat tortilla (6 in.)
1 tablespoon low-calorie mayonnaise
1 heaping tablespoon chopped fresh cilantro
2 curly lettuce leaves
1 slice low-fat processed Swiss cheese
1 cooked crab stick (1½ ozs.)
  Green Onion Tie, for garnish (directions follow)

1. Spread mayonnaise over one side of tortilla.

2. Sprinkle cilantro over mayonnaise. Follow with lettuce leaves, then position cheese slice in center of tortilla, pressing down to flatten.

3. Place crab stick at one end of tortilla and roll into a cylinder. Tie with green onion strip.

4. Serve either hot or cold. To heat, cover with waxed paper and place in microwave oven. Cook (medium) 20 seconds or until warmed.

Green Onion Tie

3 cups water
2 teaspoons salt
6 ice cubes
1 green onion

1. Combine water, salt, and ice in a medium bowl.

2. Using a pointed, sharp knife, insert tip of blade into base of green stalk, and cut up and through the end, as if it were a ribbon. Cut away the white parts.

3. Soak in salted ice water 30 minutes to 60 minutes. Stalk will become pliable and will curl like ribbon.

Nutritional Data

PER SERVING		EXCHANGES	
Calories:	230	Milk:	0.0
% Calories from fat:	29	Vegetable:	0.1
Fat (gm):	7.5	Fruit:	0.0
Sat. fat (gm):	2.4	Bread:	1.3
Cholesterol (mg):	24.7	Meat:	1.9
Sodium (mg):	590	Fat:	0.9
Protein (gm):	14.8		
Carbohydrate (gm):	27.1		

DON'T MESS WITH TEXAS BEEF ROLL

You can mess with this recipe. The name for this rolled sandwich was inspired by a thoroughly Texas bumper sticker, which is the slogan for a Texas clean-up campaign. It's fun to make and easy to eat out of hand.

Serves 3

1 cup (4 ozs.) julienned lean roast beef
½ cup salsa
½ cup chopped tomatoes
⅓ cup chopped jicama
1 jalapeño (or more, depending on your taste), finely chopped
6 spinach leaves
2 tablespoons chopped cilantro
3 whole-wheat tortillas (6 in.)
Lime wedges

1. In a medium bowl, combine beef with salsa, tomatoes, jicama, and chopped jalapeño.

2. Line each tortilla with 2 spinach leaves and sprinkle with cilantro. Spoon one-third of beef mixture on edge of each tortilla and roll up. Repeat with other 2 tortillas.

3. Tie with a Green Onion Tie, if desired (see instructions, previous recipe). Serve immediately with lime wedges, or wrap in plastic and refrigerate.

Nutritional Data

PER SERVING		EXCHANGES	
Calories:	202	Milk:	0.0
% Calories from fat:	24	Vegetable:	0.3
Fat (gm):	5.1	Fruit:	0.0
Sat. fat (gm):	1.2	Bread:	1.3
Cholesterol (mg):	27	Meat:	1.6
Sodium (mg):	494	Fat:	0.5
Protein (gm):	15.2		
Carbohydrate (gm):	22.7		

VEGETABLE SANDWICH ON CHEESE BREAD

Cheese bread just tastes rich yet is relatively low in fat. It is good for the soul to indulge in rich foods once in a while and in this low-fat sandwich, good for the body as well. Look for cheese bread at gourmet bakeries or wherever specialty breads are sold.

Serves 1

- 2 slices cheese bread, lightly toasted
- 1 tablespoon low-calorie mayonnaise
- 1½ teaspoons prepared horseradish, depending on your taste
- ¼ red, green, and/or yellow bell pepper, thinly sliced
- ¼ large fresh tomato, sliced
- 1 oz. fat-free mozzarella cheese
- 2 thin slices of red onion
- 2 tablespoons fresh parsley, chopped

1. Spread mayonnaise and horseradish over both sides of cheese toast.
2. Layer sliced bell pepper, tomato, cheese, and onions over horseradish. Sprinkle on parsley. Cover with top slice of toasted bread, dressing side down.

Nutritional Data

PER SERVING		EXCHANGES	
Calories:	224	Milk:	0.1
% Calories from fat:	18	Vegetable:	1.6
Fat (gm):	4.5	Fruit:	0.0
Sat. fat (gm):	1	Bread:	1.3
Cholesterol (mg):	27	Meat:	1.3
Sodium (mg):	564	Fat:	0.9
Protein (gm):	14.5		
Carbohydrate (gm):	32.8		

Tomato, Spinach & Cheese Burritos

A Neapolitan burrito!

Serves 4

1/2 lb. spinach
3/4 teaspoons chili powder
1/2 teaspoon crushed dried hot red chilies
1/2 teaspoon ground cumin
1 teaspoon Parmesan cheese
1 cup fat-free ricotta cheese
1 cup low-fat ricotta cheese
4 flour tortillas (8 in.)
1 large tomato, chopped
Olive-oil-flavored vegetable cooking spray
Fresh spinach leaves, for garnish
3/4 cup prepared salsa
1/2 cup nonfat sour cream

1. Preheat oven to 400 degrees. Discard wilted spinach leaves and roots; rinse leaves well and drain.

2. Coarsely shred half the spinach in a food processor. Wrap remaining spinach in towels, seal in a plastic bag, and chill.

3. Place chili powder, chilies, cumin, Parmesan cheese, and ricotta cheese in bowl of food processor. Process until smooth.

4. In center of each tortilla, layer 1/4 of the shredded spinach, ricotta mixture, and chopped tomato. Fold opposite sides over filling, then roll tortilla over and tuck open ends under it. Lay seam down in 9 x 13-in. casserole coated with vegetable spray. Repeat to fill remaining tortillas. Spray tops of burritos with vegetable spray.

5. Bake, uncovered, until golden brown, about 25 minutes. Arrange burritos on chilled spinach leaves. Spoon a stream of salsa, then sour cream, over burritos.

Nutritional Data

PER SERVING		EXCHANGES	
Calories:	192	Milk:	0.5
% Calories from fat:	27	Vegetable:	0.4
Fat (gm):	6.1	Fruit:	0.0
Sat. fat (gm):	3.4	Bread:	0.3
Cholesterol (mg):	27	Meat:	1.9
Sodium (mg):	569	Fat:	0.5
Protein (gm):	19.5		
Carbohydrate (gm):	17.4		

SALSA DOGS

Serves 4

4 low-fat frankfurters
4 whole-wheat tortillas (6 in.)
½ cup Tomato-Pineapple Salsa (recipe follows)
Nonfat sour cream, optional

1. Roast frankfurter over barbecue grill until done the way you like it.
2. Place a tortilla on grill until lightly toasted and warm; turn and toast other side. Repeat with other tortillas.
3. Remove tortillas and slightly fold in half. Fill each with salsa. Tuck frankfurter into tortilla and garnish with sour cream, if desired.

Nutritional Data (not including Tomato-Pineapple Salsa)

PER SERVING		EXCHANGES	
Calories:	201	Milk:	0.0
% Calories from fat:	22	Vegetable:	0.6
Fat (gm):	4	Fruit:	0.8
Sat. fat (gm):	0.8	Bread:	1.3
Cholesterol (mg):	15	Meat:	0.9
Sodium (mg):	650	Fat:	0.5
Protein (gm):	10.2		
Carbohydrate (gm):	31.5		

Tomato-Pineapple Salsa
Makes 4, 2-tablespoon servings

- 1 medium-size ripe tomato, diced
- ¼ cup finely diced pineapple, fresh or canned
- 1 thin green onion, thinly sliced
- 1 teaspoon minced jalapeño pepper
- 1 tablespoon minced cilantro
- 2 teaspoons lime juice
  Dash salt

1. Combine all ingredients and refrigerate until ready to serve.

Nutritional Data

PER SERVING		EXCHANGES	
Calories:	38	Milk:	0.0
% Calories from fat:	4	Vegetable:	0.6
Fat (gm):	0.1	Fruit:	0.8
Sat. fat (gm):	0	Bread:	0.0
Cholesterol (mg):	0	Meat:	0.0
Sodium (mg):	14	Fat:	0.0
Protein (gm):	1.2		
Carbohydrate (gm):	8		

EGGPLANT PESTO SANDWICH

A down-to-earth, meaty-tasting sandwich. For delightful eggplant sandwiches without the bread, use the eggplant slices as the "bread," sandwiching pesto, cheese, and tomatoes.

Serves 2

- 4 eggplant slices, ¼ in. thick
  Olive-oil-flavored vegetable cooking spray
- 4 slices calorie-reduced whole-wheat bread
- 2 tablespoons Pesto (recipe follows)
- 2 1-oz. slices fat-free mozzarella cheese
  Alfalfa sprouts
- 6 slices dried tomatoes, chopped
- 2 tablespoons nonfat mayonnaise

1. Using a sharp paring knife or vegetable peeler, cut skin off eggplant slices. In 10 to 12-in. skillet sprayed with nonstick spray, over high heat, saute eggplant slices 2 minutes on each side.

2. Lightly toast bread; spread 2 slices with 1 tablespoon pesto each. Place 2 slices of eggplant over pesto; layer mozzarella cheese and alfalfa sprouts.

3. Mix together mayonnaise and dried tomatoes. Spread mixture over remaining slices of toast, and use them to cover sandwiches.

Nutritional Data *(not including Pesto)*

PER SERVING		EXCHANGES	
Calories:	250	Milk:	0.1
% Calories from fat:	23	Vegetable:	0.1
Fat (gm):	6.4	Fruit:	0.0
Sat. fat (gm):	1.8	Bread:	2.2
Cholesterol (mg):	8.7	Meat:	1.9
Sodium (mg):	694	Fat:	2.2
Protein (gm):	16		
Carbohydrate (gm):	33.9		

Pesto
Makes 1/2 cup

1 1/2 cups fresh basil leaves, firmly packed,
   or parsley
2 tablespoons olive oil
5 garlic cloves, minced
1/4 cup Parmesan cheese

1. In food processor, combine first 3 ingredients and process until basil is finely chopped.

2. Add cheese and process until thoroughly combined. Refrigerate any excess Pesto up to 1 week to enhance future meat, cheese, or vegetable sandwiches.

Nutritional Data

PER 2-TABLESPOON SERVING		EXCHANGES	
Calories:	63	Milk:	0.0
% Calories from fat:	82	Vegetable:	0.0
Fat (gm):	5.9	Fruit:	0.0
Sat. fat (gm):	1.5	Bread:	0.0
Cholesterol (mg):	3.7	Meat:	0.3
Sodium (mg):	87	Fat:	1.0
Protein (gm):	2.2		
Carbohydrate (gm):	0.6		

ORIENTAL TUNA BURGERS

Orange, ginger, and sour cream give tuna a deliciously new dimension!

Serves 3

4 tablespoons nonfat sour cream
1 tablespoon frozen orange juice concentrate, thawed
1 teaspoon ground ginger
1 6½-oz. can tuna in water, drained, rinsed, and flaked
½ cup mandarin oranges, drained, *or* 1 medium orange, chopped
½ cup chopped red bell pepper
1 green onion (including tops), thinly sliced
2 tablespoons chopped fresh parsley
1 cup bean sprouts
3 calorie-reduced hamburger buns

1. Preheat broiler.
2. In a medium bowl, combine sour cream, orange juice concentrate, and ginger. Add tuna, oranges, bell pepper, onions, parsley, and sprouts, blending well.
3. Divide filling over bottom of hamburger buns and place on a 9 x 15-in. baking sheet. Broil tuna until bubbly. Toast tops of buns until lightly brown. Serve nice and hot.

Nutritional Data

PER SERVING		EXCHANGES	
Calories:	222	Milk:	0.1
% Calories from fat:	13	Vegetable:	0.5
Fat (gm):	3	Fruit:	0.1
Sat. fat (gm):	0.2	Bread:	1.0
Cholesterol (mg):	21	Meat:	2.5
Sodium (mg):	486	Fat:	0.3
Protein (gm):	26.2		
Carbohydrate (gm):	20		

4.
SANDWICHES
KIDS LOVE

The kitchen can be a playground, too! Make sandwiches special, using the following tricks:

Change the Shape: Flatten the bread with a rolling pin: spread filling over the bread and roll it up, jellyroll fashion. Cut roll into pinwheels. Use a scissors to cut tortillas into almost any shape, such as scallops, hearts, or letters. Do the same with pancakes, using a butter knife. Cut sandwiches into strips, tiny squares, diamonds, or other geometric shapes.

Make "Waffled Bread": Spread both sides of a slice of bread with diet margarine. Heat waffle iron according to manufacturer's directions. Insert the bread into waffle iron and close lid. Wait 2 to 3 minutes or until the bread is waffled and crisp. Dress it up with your favorite topping. "Waffle" 2 slices of bread to make a "waffled sandwich."

Make a "Checkerboard Sandwich": Prepare a sandwich using 1 slice of whole wheat and 1 slice of white bread. Cut in half, then cut each half into 2-in. squares. Turn every other square upside down to simulate a checkerboard design.

Imprint a Message: Using bits of food, such as strips of cheese, lunch meat, bell pepper, sliced olive, pimiento, raisins, berries, nuts, or jam, decorate a sandwich with a smiling face or a personal message—maybe the child's initial or a big "X" for a kiss!

Teaching Self-Reliance

Your children's lunchbox can be a backpack, a bag, canvas tote, or chartreuse lunch pail. What matters most is what's inside and for them to learn their very own lunch-making routine. With a little coaching, they will pick up good eating habits (from you, of course), which will serve them the rest of their lives.

Consult with your kids early in the planning stage before the question "what would you like?" comes up. Take them shopping and point out why such foods as turkey, chicken, and fish are good choices, for example. In casual conversation teach what makes a balanced meal. Point out how you follow the same guidelines when making dinner.

Give praise when you catch children doing something right. Show your confidence in them! Say "You did a great job on that apple," or "I have confidence in your judgment." Don't demand perfection. Point out how much he or she has mastered. Praise them by saying, "Look how much you've learned!"

Vanilla Crème Sandwich

Tastes like an ice cream sandwich! But unlike ice cream, this one is better for you because the combination of complex carbohydrates, B vitamins, and protein will stabilize blood sugar levels for hours. Sandwiching high-fiber crispbread crackers with a moist filling softens the cracker to the cake-like consistency of an ice-cream sandwich.

Serves 1

¾ cup lowfat cottage cheese
¾ teaspoon vanilla extract
2 teaspoons sugar
2 high fiber crispbread crackers (WASA Extra Fiber are good)

1. Combine cottage cheese, vanilla, and sugar in a small bowl. Evenly spread filling over entire cracker and cover sandwich with second cracker.

2. Wrap in plastic. Refrigerate 8 hours or overnight.

Nutritional Data

PER SERVING		EXCHANGES	
Calories:	192	Milk:	0.0
% Calories from fat:	11	Vegetable:	0.0
Fat (gm):	2.3	Fruit:	0.0
Sat. fat (gm):	1.4	Bread:	1.0
Cholesterol (mg):	9.5	Meat:	2.3
Sodium (mg):	511	Fat:	0.0
Protein (gm):	17.2		
Carbohydrate (gm):	24.9		

APPLE, CHEESE & A LITTLE SQUEEZE SANDWICH

"A sandwich without cheese is like a kiss without a squeeze!"

Serves 1

- 1/3 cup nonfat cottage cheese
- 1 tablespoon apple juice concentrate
- 1/4 teaspoon cinnamon
- 1/2 medium Granny Smith apple, peeled and sliced
- 1/2 teaspoon lime juice
- 2 slices raisin bread, lightly toasted
- 1/2 cup alfalfa sprouts

1. In a small bowl, combine cottage cheese, apple juice concentrate, and cinnamon; set aside. Coat apple slices with lime juice. Stack slices of bread, and trim off crusts with a butter knife.

2. Spread 1 slice of raisin toast with cottage cheese mixture. Cover with apple slices, alfalfa sprouts, and remaining slice of raisin toast. Now *S-Q-U-E-E-Z-E*.

Nutritional Data

PER SERVING		EXCHANGES	
Calories:	248	Milk:	0.0
% Calories from fat:	8	Vegetable:	0.1
Fat (gm):	2.8	Fruit:	2.1
Sat. fat (gm):	0.7	Bread:	1.4
Cholesterol (mg):	3.3	Meat:	1.4
Sodium (mg):	383	Fat:	0.3
Protein (gm):	15.1		
Carbohydrate (gm):	54.9		

FRANKFURTER STEAKS

*Don't wait to go camping. If you have a fireplace,
roast hot dogs tonight!*

Serves 4

4 low-fat frankfurters
2 medium low-sodium dill pickles, cut in half
   lengthwise
1 slice nonfat processed Swiss cheese, cut into
   4 strips
4 slices turkey bacon, *or* beef breakfast strips
4 hot dog buns

1. Slit hot dogs almost through lengthwise.

2. Stuff each hot dog with a slice of pickle and a strip of cheese. Wrap each stuffed wiener tightly with a warm bacon slice. Secure with toothpicks.

3. Roast over a hot fire until done to your preference. Remove toothpicks. Serve in buns toasted over the grill.

Nutritional Data

PER SERVING		EXCHANGES	
Calories:	174	Milk:	0.0
% Calories from fat:	28	Vegetable:	0.0
Fat (gm):	5.5	Fruit:	0.3
Sat. fat (gm):	1.1	Bread:	1.1
Cholesterol (mg):	13.7	Meat:	0.7
Sodium (mg):	590	Fat:	0.5
Protein (gm):	9.2		
Carbohydrate (gm):	23		

INSIDE-OUT HAM SANDWICH STRIPS

Serves 1

2 slices calorie-reduced white, *or* whole-wheat, bread
2 tablespoons nonfat cream cheese
1 low-sodium dill pickle, sliced diagonally into 4 pieces
2 1-oz. slices extra-lean deli ham, cut into 8 strips
4 toothpicks
4 cherry tomatoes

1. Trim crust from slices of bread.

2. Spread bread slices with cream cheese and stack them together; cut into 4 sandwich strips.

3. Tuck slice of pickle inside each strip and wrap with 2 slices of meat; fasten with a toothpick. Cover toothpick with a cherry tomato.

Nutritional Data

PER SERVING

		EXCHANGES	
Calories:	169	Milk:	0.1
% Calories from fat:	14	Vegetable:	0.0
Fat (gm):	2.7	Fruit:	0.0
Sat. fat (gm):	0.7	Bread:	1.6
Cholesterol (mg):	11	Meat:	0.9
Sodium (mg):	595	Fat:	0.2
Protein (gm):	12.4		
Carbohydrate (gm):	23.7		

SANDWICH OF MANY COLORS

Serves 1

2 slices whole-grain bread
2 tablespoons nonfat cream cheese
1 tablespoon no-sugar-added fruit spread, such
   as strawberry, grape, boysenberry, blueberry,
   apple butter (use any combination)
   Handful of fresh berries, such as raspberries,
   blueberries, and/or strawberries

1. Spread cream cheese over 1 slice of bread.
2. Dot different jams and apple butter over the cheese in a pattern that appeals to you (using your fingers if you wish). Press in the berries.
3. Cover with second slice of bread. Cut into fancy shapes.

Nutritional Data

PER SERVING		EXCHANGES	
Calories:	182	Milk:	0.2
% Calories from fat:	11	Vegetable:	0.0
Fat (gm):	2	Fruit:	0.5
Sat. fat (gm):	0.4	Bread:	1.6
Cholesterol (mg):	5	Meat:	0.0
Sodium (mg):	435	Fat:	0.4
Protein (gm):	8.7		
Carbohydrate (gm):	30.8		

HAMNANNERS

Eat these with a good honey mustard.

Serves 5

1 pkg. (7½ ozs., 10 biscuits) refrigerated biscuits
¾ cup finely diced celery

5   ozs. extra-lean sliced ham
1   large banana, thinly sliced
1   tablespoon + 2 teaspoons toasted wheat germ
1/4 cup low-fat milk
1   tablespoon poppyseeds
    Vegetable cooking spray

1. Preheat oven to 450 degrees. Roll each biscuit into a 5-in. circle.
2. Sprinkle 5 biscuits with diced celery and cover with slices of ham, trimming fat if necessary. Arrange banana slices over ham; sprinkle each round with 1 teaspoon wheat germ.
3. Moisten edges of dough rounds with water. Top each with another dough round and press edges together with your fingers, making a fluted edge. Brush tops with milk; sprinkle with poppyseeds.
4. Coat a 12 x 15-in. baking sheet with nonstick vegetable spray. Set Hamnanners on baking sheet. Bake 15 minutes or until golden brown.

Nutritional Data

PER SERVING		EXCHANGES	
Calories:	171	Milk:	0.0
% Calories from fat:	18	Vegetable:	0.0
Fat (gm):	3.5	Fruit:	0.4
Sat. fat (gm):	0.1	Bread:	1.5
Cholesterol (mg):	15	Meat:	0.8
Sodium (mg):	592	Fat:	0.7
Protein (gm):	8		
Carbohydrate (gm):	27.7		

TEA PARTY SANDWICHES

Get out the children's tea set and enjoy an "afternoon tea."

Serves 3

6   tablespoons (3 ozs.) fat-free cream cheese
6   slices raisin bread, crusts removed
1   cup sliced fresh fruit, such as strawberries, peaches, kiwi, bananas, grapes, and/or apples

1. Spread one side of all bread slices with cream cheese. Cut each slice into 2 triangles.
2. Arrange fruit slices in a pretty pattern over the cream cheese.

Nutritional Data

PER SERVING		EXCHANGES	
Calories:	208	Milk:	0.0
% Calories from fat:	30	Vegetable:	0.0
Fat (gm):	7.2	Fruit:	0.0
Sat. fat (gm):	3.5	Bread:	1.8
Cholesterol (mg):	9.9	Meat:	0.0
Sodium (mg):	362	Fat:	1.3
Protein (gm):	7.4		
Carbohydrate (gm):	30.4		

SWISS SHREDDED WHEAT SANDWICH

Serves 1

1 Shredded Wheat biscuit
2 tablespoons nonfat sour cream
1/2 cup raspberries, or blueberries
1 tablespoon slivered almonds
1 slice nonfat processed Swiss cheese

1. Using a sharp knife, slice open biscuit horizontally.
2. Spoon sour cream into hollow case. Layer berries and almonds over sour cream and cover with slice of cheese.
3. Replace "lid" over bottom biscuit and microwave (high) 30 seconds. Serve hot.

Nutritional Data

PER SERVING		EXCHANGES	
Calories:	195	Milk:	0.1
% Calories from fat:	28	Vegetable:	1.0
Fat (gm):	6.8	Fruit:	0.2
Sat. fat (gm):	2.3	Bread:	1.0
Cholesterol (mg):	10	Meat:	1.0
Sodium (mg):	341	Fat:	0.8
Protein (gm):	12.6		
Carbohydrate (gm):	27		

STRAWBERRY PIZZA

Kids between the ages of 3 and 11 prefer pizza over all other foods for lunch and dinner, according to a recent Gallup poll. They (and you) will love this one even more—and it's low in fat, too!

Serves 5

1 pkg. (7½ ozs., 10 biscuits) refrigerated biscuits
1 orange
1 pkg. (8 ozs.) fat-free cream cheese
4 teaspoons honey, divided
1 pt. basket, *or* 3¼ cups (12 to 14 ozs.), strawberries, stemmed, and halved
   Mint sprigs, for garnish

1. Preheat oven to 400 degrees.
2. Stack 2 biscuits; roll out to a circle about 6 in. in diameter, ⅛ in. thick. Place on ungreased baking sheet. Prick all with fork. Repeat with remaining biscuits to make a total of 5 circles. Bake until lightly browned, 6 to 8 minutes. Loosen biscuits and cool slightly.
3. Meanwhile, finely grate peel of orange into a bowl. Add cheese and 2 teaspoons honey and blend thoroughly; set aside.
4. Juice orange into another bowl. Add strawberries and the remaining 2 teaspoons of honey; toss. Increase oven temperature to 425 degrees.
5. Spread biscuits with cheese mixture to within ½-in. of edges, dividing equally. Bake just until edges of cheese brown lightly. Top with drained

strawberries. Garnish with mint sprigs. Serve immediately to your anxiously awaiting audience!

Nutritional Data

PER SERVING		EXCHANGES	
Calories:	221	Milk:	0.3
% Calories from fat:	9	Vegetable:	0.0
Fat (gm):	2.2	Fruit:	0.2
Sat. fat (gm):	0	Bread:	1.4
Cholesterol (mg):	7.9	Meat:	0.0
Sodium (mg):	578	Fat:	0.4
Protein (gm):	9.2		
Carbohydrate (gm):	41.4		

SUNSHINE TOAST

Serves 3

1 cup nonfat cottage cheese
3 tablespoons orange juice
1 teaspoon Dijon-style mustard
2 teaspoons honey
3 slices calorie-reduced oat bran bread, toasted
2 tablespoons chopped dry-roasted peanuts

1. Combine cottage cheese, orange juice, mustard, and honey in a blender. Process until smooth, stopping blender often to scrape sides. (Or, instead of blender, the children can simply stir ingredients together.)

2. Spread cottage cheese mixture over each slice of toast. Sprinkle each with 2 teaspoons chopped peanuts.

Nutritional Data

PER SERVING		EXCHANGES	
Calories:	158	Milk:	0.0
% Calories from fat:	21	Vegetable:	0.0
Fat (gm):	3.9	Fruit:	0.1
Sat. fat (gm):	0.5	Bread:	0.8
Cholesterol (mg):	3.3	Meat:	1.6
Sodium (mg):	472	Fat:	0.6
Protein (gm):	13.8		
Carbohydrate (gm):	19.3		

SPICED PEMMICAN BUNS

Native Americans preserved buffalo and venison with fat, spices, and fruit. Small cowboys and Indians prefer this.

Serves 4

- ½ cup plain yogurt
- 1 teaspoon mustard
- 1 teaspoon honey
- ⅛ teaspoon each: ground cinnamon, allspice, and cloves
- ¼ cup golden raisins
- 1 cup chopped apple
- *1 cup finely chopped roast buffalo, *or* lean venison
- 4 calorie-reduced whole-wheat hamburger buns, toasted

1. In a medium bowl, combine yogurt, mustard, honey, and spices. Stir in raisins, chopped apple, and chopped meat. Toss to coat.
2. Fill buns to the brim.

*Chopped turkey, chicken, or beef may be substituted.

Nutritional Data

PER SERVING		EXCHANGES	
Calories:	225	Milk:	0.2
% Calories from fat:	11	Vegetable:	0.0
Fat (gm):	2.7	Fruit:	1.4
Sat. fat (gm):	0.4	Bread:	0.9
Cholesterol (mg):	21	Meat:	1.0
Sodium (mg):	271	Fat:	0.2
Protein (gm):	14		
Carbohydrate (gm):	37.6		

TUNA AT THE WALDORF

Serves 3

1 6½ oz. can tuna in water, rinsed, drained, and flaked
1 small apple, chopped
½ stalk celery, chopped
1 tablespoon walnuts, finely chopped
½ cup nonfat sour cream
2 teaspoons prepared mustard
3 English muffin halves with raisins, toasted

1. Combine all ingredients in a small bowl and spread over English muffin halves. That's all!

Nutritional Data

PER SERVING		EXCHANGES	
Calories:	244	Milk:	0.1
% Calories from fat:	12	Vegetable:	0.0
Fat (gm):	3.2	Fruit:	1.2
Sat. fat (gm):	0.5	Bread:	0.8
Cholesterol (mg):	18	Meat:	2.2
Sodium (mg):	354	Fat:	0.4
Protein (gm):	21.2		
Carbohydrate (gm):	33.7		

STRAWBERRY BANANA BURROS

Serves 4

½ cup part-skim ricotta cheese
¼ teaspoon ground cinnamon
1 tablespoon brown sugar
4 whole-wheat tortillas (6-in.)

4 tablespoons no-sugar-added strawberry jam
4 small bananas

1. In a small bowl, combine ricotta, cinnamon, and sugar; mix well.

2. Spread about 2 tablespoons mixture over each tortilla. Add a layer of strawberry jam over the cheese mixture.

3. Peel bananas and place on one edge of each tortilla; roll up. Eat as is, or cut into pinwheels.

Nutritional Data

PER SERVING		EXCHANGES	
Calories:	245	Milk:	0.2
% Calories from fat:	10	Vegetable:	0.0
Fat (gm):	2.9	Fruit:	1.8
Sat. fat (gm):	0.5	Bread:	1.5
Cholesterol (mg):	3	Meat:	0.4
Sodium (mg):	184	Fat:	0.5
Protein (gm):	7.9		
Carbohydrate (gm):	49.9		

SWEETIE PIES

Have your pie and eat it, too! Nonfat cream cheese provides a respectable amount of protein. Blueberries and whole-wheat tortillas supply 3 grams of dietary fiber!

Serves 2

Vegetable cooking spray
2 whole-wheat tortillas (6 in.)
1/4 cup (2 ozs.) nonfat cream cheese
1/4 cup fresh fruit, such as blueberries, sliced strawberries, peaches, and/or kiwi
2 teaspoons cinnamon-sugar (combination of 1 3/4 teaspoons sugar and 1/4 teaspoon cinnamon)
Powdered sugar, for garnish

1. Coat an 8-in. nonstick skillet with vegetable spray and set over medium heat. Place 1 tortilla in skillet.

2. Spread half of tortilla with 2 tablespoons of cream cheese. Press in half the fruit, sprinkle with cinnamon-sugar, and fold tortilla in half. Pan fry 2 minutes on each side. Dust with powdered sugar.

3. Repeat with remaining tortilla.

Nutritional Data

PER SERVING		EXCHANGES	
Calories:	174	Milk:	0.2
% Calories from fat:	27	Vegetable:	0.0
Fat (gm):	4.9	Fruit:	0.2
Sat. fat (gm):	0.3	Bread:	1.3
Cholesterol (mg):	5	Meat:	0.0
Sodium (mg):	337	Fat:	1.0
Protein (gm):	7.2		
Carbohydrate (gm):	23.6		

COCOA-CINNAMON TOAST

Serves 1

1 slice raisin bread, lightly toasted
1 pat (teaspoon) diet margarine
2 teaspoons instant sugar-free cocoa mix
1/8 teaspoon cinnamon

1. Spread one side of toast with margarine, covering entire surface.

2. Place toast, margarine-side up, on sheet of foil or tray of toaster-oven. Combine cocoa mix and cinnamon; sprinkle evenly over toast. Broil 3 inches from heat source, about 1 minute, until bubbly and dark brown.

Nutritional Data

PER SERVING		EXCHANGES	
Calories:	90	Milk:	0.0
% Calories from fat:	30	Vegetable:	0.0
Fat (gm):	3	Fruit:	0.0
Sat. fat (gm):	0.6	Bread:	0.9
Cholesterol (mg):	14	Meat:	0.0
Sodium (mg):	155	Fat:	0.5
Protein (gm):	2.3		
Carbohydrate (gm):	14.2		

Fruit, Ham & Cheese Roll-Ups

Serves 4

⅔ cup crushed pineapple in juice, drained
½ cup fat-free ricotta cheese
4 1-oz slices lean ham
4 curly lettuce leaves
4 calorie-reduced hot dog buns

1. Combine pineapple and ricotta cheese.
2. Overlap 2 ham slices, making length same as length of hot dog bun.
3. Spoon 3 tablespoons of pineapple-cheese mixture along one edge of ham, then roll up, enclosing fruit. Place a lettuce leaf in each bun; cover with the "roll-up."

Nutritional Data

PER SERVING		EXCHANGES	
Calories:	155	Milk:	0.2
% Calories from fat:	13	Vegetable:	0.0
Fat (gm):	2.2	Fruit:	0.4
Sat. fat (gm):	0	Bread:	0.9
Cholesterol (mg):	18	Meat:	1.1
Sodium (mg):	465	Fat:	0.5
Protein (gm):	13.2		
Carbohydrate (gm):	21.5		

DOUBLE HONEY SANDWICH STACKS

Winnie The Pooh would approve of these.

Serves 2

4 teaspoons diet margarine, softened
1 tablespoon honey
2 slices calorie-reduced whole-wheat bread
2 slices calorie-reduced white bread
3 slices honey loaf, *or* honey ham
6 small unsalted pretzel sticks

1. Make "honey butter" by stirring together the softened margarine and honey in a small bowl until thoroughly combined.

2. Stack all 4 slices of bread, alternating whole-wheat and white slices. Spread about 2 teaspoons of honey butter between each layer. Place 1 slice of meat between each slice of bread.

3. Cut sandwich stack into 3 rectangles. Cut each rectangle in half, cross-wise, making 6 small sandwiches. Spear each sandwich with a pretzel stick.

Nutritional Data

PER SERVING		EXCHANGES	
Calories:	181	Milk:	0.0
% Calories from fat:	26	Vegetable:	0.0
Fat (gm):	5.7	Fruit:	0.0
Sat. fat (gm):	0.9	Bread:	1.4
Cholesterol (mg):	15	Meat:	0.7
Sodium (mg):	545	Fat:	1.1
Protein (gm):	9		
Carbohydrate (gm):	27.1		

SKINNY BOLOGNA SANDWICH

A childhood favorite for many, bologna is considered a comfort food. Whether fried or just "smashed" in a sandwich, bologna is still high in fat by today's standards—but it is also important to spoil ourselves occasionally.

Serves 1

2 slices calorie-reduced white bread
2 teaspoons mustard
2 teaspoons calorie-reduced mayonnaise
1 slice reduced-fat bologna
1 iceberg lettuce leaf

1. Spread one slice of bread with mustard and the other with mayonnaise.

2. Cover one piece of bread with bologna slice followed by lettuce; cover it with the other slice. Eat as is or press it between your palms, letting the mayo and mustard ooze out

Variation: Fried Bologna Sandwich: Saute bologna slowly over low heat until browned in a nonstick skillet coated with vegetable spray. Turn and brown other side. Use fried bologna to make the sandwich above.

Nutritional Data

PER SERVING		EXCHANGES	
Calories:	147	Milk:	0.0
% Calories from fat:	25	Vegetable:	0.0
Fat (gm):	3.9	Fruit:	0.0
Sat. fat (gm):	0.8	Bread:	1.4
Cholesterol (mg):	16	Meat:	1.5
Sodium (mg):	600	Fat:	0.5
Protein (gm):	4.5		
Carbohydrate (gm):	22.4		

DIPLOMAS

Mark the passing of kindergarten with special little "graduation" sandwiches resembling diplomas.

Serves 2

6 slices calorie-reduced white bread
2 tablespoons diet margarine
2 ozs. (6 slices) deli thin-sliced ham
6 pieces of curling ribbon

1. Trim crusts from bread; cut slices in half. Flatten with a rolling pin.
2. Spread one side of bread with diet margarine; trim slices of ham to fit bread. Arrange meat slices on top of coated bread.
3. From one end, roll up, pinwheel style. Tie with curling ribbon, closing with a bow.

Nutritional Data

PER SERVING		EXCHANGES	
Calories:	170	Milk:	0.0
% Calories from fat:	29	Vegetable:	0.0
Fat (gm):	6	Fruit:	0.0
Sat. fat (gm):	0.9	Bread:	1.4
Cholesterol (mg):	20	Meat:	0.9
Sodium (mg):	597	Fat:	1.2
Protein (gm):	10.7		
Carbohydrate (gm):	21.1		

Cottage Cheese and Cherry Toastie

Use an electric sandwich maker, a Toastie Maker, or simply grill the conventional way, using nonstick vegetable spray and a skillet.

Serves 1

¹/₂ cup nonfat cottage cheese
 1 tablespoon no-sugar-added cherry preserves
   Worcestershire sauce, few drops
 2 slices calorie-reduced white, *or* whole-wheat, bread
¹/₂ cup alfalfa sprouts
 2 teaspoons diet margarine, *or* vegetable cooking spray

1. In a small bowl, thoroughly combine cottage cheese and cherry preserves. Season to taste with a few drops of Worcestershire sauce.

2. Spoon filling between slices of bread and stuff with sprouts. Toast, using one of the following methods:

Instructions for using an Automatic Toastie Maker: Insert sandwich and toast 3 to 4 minutes or until golden brown.

Instructions for using a Hand-held Toastie Maker: Spread diet margarine over one side of both slices of bread. Prepare sandwich, buttered sides facing out. Heat over high flame until bread is golden and filling is warm, approximately 3 minutes each side.

Instructions for stove-top method: Coat a nonstick skillet with vegetable cooking spray. Grill sandwich over medium heat 2 to 3 minutes until bread is lightly toasted. Turn over and grill other side until done.

Nutritional Data

PER SERVING		EXCHANGES	
Calories:	227	Milk:	0.0
% Calories from fat:	19	Vegetable:	0.1
Fat (gm):	5.1	Fruit:	0.5
Sat. fat (gm):	0.9	Bread:	1.4
Cholesterol (mg):	5	Meat:	2.1
Sodium (mg):	590	Fat:	0.9
Protein (gm):	19.7		
Carbohydrate (gm):	29.6		

BERRY GOOD TOASTIE

Serves 1

¼ cup low-fat cottage cheese
2 slices calorie-reduced oatmeal, *or* white, bread
   Handful of blueberries, raspberries, blackber-
   ries, strawberries, or grapes
   Apple pie spice
2 teaspoons diet margarine, *or* vegetable cooking spray

1. Spread cottage cheese over 1 slice of bread. Press fruit into cottage cheese and dust with apple pie spice. Cover with second bread slice.

2. Toast sandwich, using one of the methods described on p. 102.

Variation: Use low-sugar grape jam, raisins and/or carob chips.

Nutritional Data

PER SERVING		EXCHANGES	
Calories:	150	Milk:	0.0
% Calories from fat:	11	Vegetable:	0.0
Fat (gm):	1.9	Fruit:	0.0
Sat. fat (gm):	0.6	Bread:	1.4
Cholesterol (mg):	2.5	Meat:	1.0
Sodium (mg):	439	Fat:	0.2
Protein (gm):	11.4		
Carbohydrate (gm):	24.4		

FRUITWICHES

Serves 2

3 slices egg, *or* raisin, bread
½ cup low-fat ricotta cheese
½ ripe medium banana, thinly sliced
½ cup fresh peaches, cherries, or strawberries
   Light whipping cream, optional
1 tablespoon chopped nuts, optional

1. Spread bread slices with ricotta cheese. Cover with banana slices.

2. Reserve 2 slices of fruit or whole berries for garnish; chop the remaining fruit. Sprinkle over banana slices.

3. Cut each slice of bread in an "x" pattern, making 4 triangles. Arrange in a pinwheel pattern. Garnish center of pinwheel with a fresh strawberry, cherry, or peach slice. Spray light whipping cream over fruit and sprinkle with chopped nuts (optional but highly desirable).

Nutritional Data

PER SERVING		EXCHANGES	
Calories:	228	Milk:	0.0
% Calories from fat:	26	Vegetable:	0.0
Fat (gm):	6.7	Fruit:	0.4
Sat. fat (gm):	2.8	Bread:	1.4
Cholesterol (mg):	19	Meat:	1.0
Sodium (mg):	229	Fat:	0.7
Protein (gm):	10.7		
Carbohydrate (gm):	32.1		

PUZZLE SANDWICH

Serves 1

1 slice each: calorie-reduced whole-wheat and white bread
2 tablespoons nonfat cream cheese, softened
1 tablespoon reduced-fat peanut butter
2 teaspoons seedless raisins
Sandwich cutter or sharp knife

1. Stack slices of bread together. Using a 1½-in. high sandwich cutter or knife, cut out a favorite shape from both slices of bread. (Suggestions: child's first initial, heart, diamond, star, etc.)

2. Press cut-out back into bread slices. Spread one slice with cream cheese followed by peanut butter. Sprinkle raisins over filling; cover with remaining slice.

3. Gently push out the cut-out shape and serve it with sandwich. Have the lucky recipient fill in the missing puzzle piece.

Variations: Substitute diet margarine or whipped cream cheese with one of these combinations: soft Cheddar cheese spread combined with chopped ham; peanut butter and no-sugar-added jam; yogurt and wheat germ.

Nutritional Data

PER SERVING		EXCHANGES	
Calories:	186	Milk:	0.2
% Calories from fat:	28	Vegetable:	0.0
Fat (gm):	5.8	Fruit:	0.3
Sat. fat (gm):	1.1	Bread:	1.7
Cholesterol (mg):	5	Meat:	0.0
Sodium (mg):	349	Fat:	1.3
Protein (gm):	10.2		
Carbohydrate (gm):	23.4		

COOKIE-CUTTER SPICE CAKES

Serves 2

2 slices each: calorie-reduced white and whole-wheat bread

4 teaspoons chunky peanut butter

4 tablespoons vanilla nonfat yogurt

2 tablespoons Dessert Spice (recipe follows), *or* candy sprinkles

1. Cover 1 slice of white bread with 1 slice of wheat bread. Using your favorite cookie cutter, or a sharp knife, cut shape or geometric design into the two stacked slices, such as a simple square, an octagon, a heart, or a diamond shape. Repeat with other 2 slices. (Reserve bread scraps for breadcrumbs or to feed to the birds.)

2. Spread one side of white bread cut-outs with peanut butter and one side of wheat bread cut-outs with one-half of the yogurt. Press together the peanut butter and yogurt sides of the cut-outs.

3. Spoon remaining 2 tablespoons of yogurt into small, shallow bowl. Dip all sides of cut-out sandwiches into yogurt, then into Dessert Spice, coating all edges with sweet spices.

Dessert Spice

1 tablespoon ground cinnamon
2 tablespoons sugar
1 tablespoon plus 1 teaspoon sugar-free cocoa mix
2 teaspoons grated orange rind

1. Combine all ingredients in a jar; shake to mix thoroughly. Transfer to small bowl.

Optional ingredients to add to Dessert Spice: unsweetened coconut, wheat germ, chopped dried fruit, chopped nuts, raisins, sunflower seeds, powdered brewer's yeast.

Nutritional Data

PER SERVING		EXCHANGES	
Calories:	200	Milk:	0.2
% Calories from fat:	22	Vegetable:	0.0
Fat (gm):	5.2	Fruit:	0.0
Sat. fat (gm):	0.9	Bread:	2.1
Cholesterol (mg):	0.6	Meat:	0.0
Sodium (mg):	278	Fat:	1.0
Protein (gm):	8.2		
Carbohydrate (gm):	34.2		

SUNDAE SAMWICH

A banana split in a "Samwich."

Serves 2

1 small ripe banana, thinly sliced
1 teaspoon lemon juice
1/2 cup nonfat vanilla yogurt
1 packet diet cocoa mix
1/2 cup plus 2 tablespoons low-fat ricotta cheese

4 slices calorie-reduced white bread

2 tablespoons no-sugar-added strawberry preserves

1. Sprinkle banana slices with lemon juice. Set aside.

2. Stir cocoa mix into yogurt. Add ricotta cheese and stir until well blended. Spread half the cocoa cheese mixture over 2 slices of bread. Arrange banana slices over the cheese.

3. Spread strawberry preserves over remaining bread slices; then place strawberry side down over filling, making a Sundae Samwich.

Nutritional Data

PER SERVING		EXCHANGES	
Calories:	244	Milk:	0.8
% Calories from fat:	5	Vegetable:	0.0
Fat (gm):	1.5	Fruit:	1.4
Sat. fat (gm):	0.3	Bread:	1.4
Cholesterol (mg):	8	Meat:	0.9
Sodium (mg):	282	Fat:	0.2
Protein (gm):	17		
Carbohydrate (gm):	47.8		

TUNA BOATS

Stuff a hot dog bun with traditional tuna salad, and shape it to look like a fish!

Serves 2

$1/3$ cup fat-free Ranch salad dressing

1 tablespoon sweet pickle relish

$1/4$ cup finely chopped celery

1 $6^{1}/_{2}$-oz. can tuna in water, rinsed, drained, and flaked

2 calorie-reduced hot dog buns

1 pimiento-stuffed olive, sliced in half

1. Blend dressing, pickle relish, and celery. Stir in tuna.

2. Carefully open bun and spoon in filling. Press closed slightly. Firmly encircle bun with thumb and forefinger, one-third distance from the

end. Press to indent, forming a "tail fin." Using a sharp knife, scrape crust off top tail section.

3. Holding bun right side up, poke a hole where the eyes are to be and stuff in olive slices. Create a smiling fish by carefully sawing an upturned mouth with pointed end of paring knife. Lift off crust.

Nutritional Data

PER SERVING		EXCHANGES	
Calories:	210	Milk:	0.0
% Calories from fat:	10	Vegetable:	0.0
Fat (gm):	2.3	Fruit:	0.0
Sat. fat (gm):	0.2	Bread:	1.2
Cholesterol (mg):	28	Meat:	3.4
Sodium (mg):	622	Fat:	0.2
Protein (gm):	28.5		
Carbohydrate (gm):	16.4		

SAUCY DOGS

Spread some good whole-grain or Dijon-style mustard over these sweet-and-sour dogs.

Serves 8

1   15-oz. can peaches in juice, drained
2   teaspoons Worcestershire sauce
2   teaspoons brown sugar
2½ tablespoons cider vinegar
2   teaspoons dark rum extract (non-alcoholic)
    Dash cinnamon
8   low-fat frankfurters
8   calorie-reduced hot dog buns

1. Puree peaches in food processor or blender until smooth. Add Worcestershire sauce, sugar, vinegar, rum extract, and cinnamon to the peaches and process, just to combine.

2. Pour peach mixture into a 1-quart saucepan and heat gently, stirring until simmering. Remove from heat.

3. Cook frankfurters over an electric grill or charcoal fire, basting with sauce. Turn and baste frequently until hot (about 5 minutes). Place each frankfurter in a bun. Heat remaining sauce and spoon over frankfurters before serving.

Compare amounts of fat in frankfurters made from different meats:

	Calories	Fat Grams
Beef	180	16.3
Turkey	100	8.1
Chicken	116	8.8
Low fat	70	2.0

Nutritional Data

PER SERVING		EXCHANGES	
Calories:	140	Milk:	0.0
% Calories from fat:	19	Vegetable:	0.0
Fat (gm):	3	Fruit:	0.1
Sat. fat (gm):	0.5	Bread:	0.9
Cholesterol (mg):	15	Meat:	0.9
Sodium (mg):	596	Fat:	0.2
Protein (gm):	10.4		
Carbohydrate (gm):	23.7		

5.

SUPPER SANDWICHES

D ress up a sandwich for supper or dinner and serve it proudly. Don't think, "It's just a sandwich." Even peanut butter and jelly can be elegant smothering a toasted cinnamon bagel and served on your finest china. By taking the extra time to make food attractive, loved ones will feel "fussed over." But best of all, the meal will actually *taste* better because eating at it's best is a sensual, aesthetic experience.

Here are five ways to dress up a sandwich:

1. Stuff with delicate spring greens, spread on pestos, adorn with roasted vegetables and fresh herbs.
2. Cut in fancy shapes, using cookie cutters or a sharp knife.
3. Instead of mayonnaise, use salsa or exotic relishes.
4. Cut in quarters, trim off crusts, and thread onto wooden skewers. Insert cherry tomatoes, olives, or grapes between sandwich quarters.
5. Instead of plain white bread, try something more interesting such as baguettes, bagels, crepes, a whole-wheat tortilla or heart-shaped lavosh.

GOAT'S CHEESE PILLOWS

Keep the husky flavor of goat's cheese without the fat! Wonderful as an appetizer or as a delicate first course.

Serves 1

2 ozs. (4 tablespoons) soft goat's cheese
⅓ cup nonfat cottage cheese
2 tablespoons dried tomato halves, reconstituted, chopped
 Olive-oil-flavored vegetable cooking spray
2 corn tortillas, preferably blue corn
1 tablespoon fresh mint, chopped
 Alfalfa sprouts, for garnish

1. Combine goat's cheese with cottage cheese and chopped dried tomatoes.

2. Coat a 12-in. nonstick skillet with vegetable cooking spray and set over medium heat. When skillet is hot, place tortillas in pan and heat about 1 minute; flip and heat another minute. Remove from heat.

3. Arrange half the cheese mixture over half the surface of each tortilla; sprinkle with mint.

4. Press alfalfa sprouts into cheese. After about 1 minute, fold tortilla over to close. Place lid on skillet and heat "pillows" several minutes. Remove from heat and serve immediately.

Nutritional Data

PER SERVING		EXCHANGES	
Calories:	192	Milk:	0.0
% Calories from fat:	24	Vegetable:	0.2
Fat (gm):	5.2	Fruit:	0.0
Sat. fat (gm):	3	Bread:	0.8
Cholesterol (mg):	14.7	Meat:	2.7
Sodium (mg):	422	Fat:	0.7
Protein (gm):	21.3		
Carbohydrate (gm):	16.2		

LIGHT PIEROGIS

Phyllo is light, flaky, paper-thin sheets of dough best known as the primary ingredient of Greek pastries such as baklava—but don't let it stop there! Its possibilities are almost as limitless as your own. Find phyllo in your grocer's freezer section.

Serves 2

2 12 x 17-in. phyllo dough sheets
   Butter-flavored vegetable cooking spray
1 cup Cabbage and Ham, *or* Cottage Cheese,
   Filling (recipes follow)

1. Preheat oven to 375 degrees.

2. Spray phyllo dough and fold in half (it will measure 12 x 8½-in.); spray again.

3. Measure 1 cup of filling and spread in center of rectangle. Fold dough in half, covering filling. Turn edges over to form a half circle.

4. Spray with vegetable spray, adhering edges. Repeat with other sheet of phyllo.

5. Set pierogis on a nonstick baking sheet coated with vegetable cooking spray. Bake for 15 to 20 minutes or until golden brown.

Cabbage and Ham Filling

   Vegetable cooking spray
½ onion, peeled, finely chopped
¾ cup finely chopped cabbage
2 tablespoons water
½ cup sauerkraut, drained and rinsed
½ cup chopped roasted lean ham
1 teaspoon caraway seed
¼ teaspoon pepper
¼ teaspoon marjoram

1. Coat a small skillet with nonstick vegetable spray. Saute onion and cabbage in water over medium heat until barely soft, about 6 minutes.

2. In a small bowl, combine remaining ingredients, mixing herbs thoroughly through sauerkraut. Lower heat, add sauerkraut mixture to skillet, and cook until heated through.

3. Fill pierogis as directed above.

Note: Simply rinsing sauerkraut will eliminate half the sodium!

Nutritional Data *(with Cabbage and Ham Filling)*

PER SERVING		EXCHANGES	
Calories:	160	Milk:	0.0
% Calories from fat:	12	Vegetable:	2.0
Fat (gm):	2.2	Fruit:	0.0
Sat. fat (gm):	0.6	Bread:	0.8
Cholesterol (mg):	19	Meat:	0.8
Sodium (mg):	573	Fat:	0.2
Protein (gm):	19.1		
Carbohydrate (gm):	18.4		

Cottage Cheese Filling

1   cup 2% cottage cheese
1   high-fiber crispbread cracker, crushed
1   egg-white
1/2 teaspoon salt-free herb blend, *or* 1/2 teaspoon
    dried dill weed
    Pinch garlic powder, optional

1. Combine all ingredients in a bowl and mix well. Fill pierogis as directed.

Nutritional Data *(with Cottage Cheese Filling)*

PER SERVING		EXCHANGES	
Calories:	186	Milk:	0.0
% Calories from fat:	16	Vegetable:	0.0
Fat (gm):	3.3	Fruit:	0.0
Sat. fat (gm):	1.5	Bread:	1.0
Cholesterol (mg):	9.5	Meat:	2.5
Sodium (mg):	591	Fat:	0.2
Protein (gm):	17.7		
Carbohydrate (gm):	9.5		

Hot Dogs En Croûte with Mexican Corn Salsa

♦

Anything under wraps is a mystery, therefore more desirable.
Phyllo dough can add glamour to a plain hot dog, particularly
when encased with Mexican Corn Salsa.

Serves 4

1⅓ cups Mexican Corn Salsa (recipe follows)
4 sheets phyllo dough
Butter-flavored vegetable cooking spray
4 low-fat hot dogs

1. Prepare Mexican Corn Salsa: set aside. Preheat oven to 350 degrees. Thaw phyllo according to package directions. Take care to keep phyllo covered with a slightly damp towel, and spray it liberally with vegetable spray to prevent it from drying out.

2. Unroll phyllo dough and remove 1 sheet. Cover roll of phyllo dough with damp towel. Spray entire sheet of phyllo with vegetable spray. Fold both outside edges inward approximately 4 inches.

3. Place hot dog in center of dough and cover with ⅓ cup Mexican Corn Salsa. Spray dough with vegetable spray again. Fold both ends of dough over hot dog, forming a package. Tuck dough under and spray once more. Repeat with remaining sheets of dough and hot dogs.

4. Spray baking sheet with vegetable spray. Transfer packages to sheet. Bake 20 minutes or until crisp and golden brown.

Note: Before returning unused phyllo dough to refrigerator, spray with vegetable spray, particularly the edges to protect against drying out.

Fun Variations: Think of a sheet of phyllo as a piece of wrapping paper. Feel free to form interesting packaging such as **The Candywrap:** fold phyllo in half lengthwise. Center hot dog at one end of sheet and roll up. Spray with vegetable spray and cinch both ends shut by pinching your fingers, to resemble a wrapped piece of hard candy.

Mexican Corn Salsa
Makes 3½ cups

1 cup diced red bell pepper
1 cup diced green bell pepper
1 cup frozen corn, thawed
1 jalapeño pepper, seeded finely chopped (wear rubber gloves and avoid contact with eyes)
½ cup chopped onion
1 garlic clove, minced
1 tablespoon Dijon-style mustard
1 tablespoon vegetable oil
1 tablespoon fresh lime juice
1 tablespoon chopped fresh cilantro

1. Combine all ingredients in a bowl. Mix well and chill in refrigerator.

Nutritional Data

PER SERVING		EXCHANGES	
Calories:	135	Milk:	0.0
% Calories from fat:	25	Vegetable:	0.5
Fat (gm):	3.7	Fruit:	0.0
Sat. fat (gm):	0.7	Bread:	0.8
Cholesterol (mg):	15	Meat:	0.9
Sodium (mg):	578	Fat:	0.4
Protein (gm):	8		
Carbohydrate (gm):	18.5		

ITALIAN EGGPLANT ROLLS WITH MARINARA SAUCE

During World War II, meat was rationed and sometimes eggplant was substituted. It was often referred to as the "poor man's pork chop." These rolls "sandwich" a lovely, light Italian filling. Or put it on a slice of bread, if you like.

Serves 3 (2 rolls each)

- ³/₄ cup low-fat ricotta cheese
- 1 teaspoon Italian seasoning
- 3 tablespoons grated Parmesan cheese
- 1¹/₂ tablespoons cut up sun-dried tomatoes
- 1 eggplant, 6–8 in. long
- 6 spinach leaves, rinsed and dried
- ¹/₂ cup Marinara Sauce (recipe follows), *or* purchased
- 1 tablespoon chopped fresh parsley

1. In a small bowl, combine ricotta cheese, Italian seasoning, and Parmesan cheese; mix well. Stir in sun-dried tomatoes.

2. Slice eggplant *lengthwise* into 6, ¹/₈-in. wide slices. Wrap eggplant in microwave-safe paper towels and microwave (high) 1 minute or until soft. Set aside to cool.

3. Spread about 2¹/₂ tablespoons of cheese mixture over each eggplant slice. Place spinach leaves over cheese and roll up like a jellyroll. Keep roll closed by inserting toothpicks into eggplant.

4. Arrange rolls side by side on serving plate. Pour a stream of Marinara Sauce, about ¹/₂ cup total, down center of eggplant rolls. Garnish with chopped parsley.

Marinara Sauce
Makes 2 cups

- ¹/₂ cup finely chopped onion
- ¹/₂ cup finely chopped bell pepper
- 2 cups no-salt-added vegetable juice cocktail, divided
- 1 teaspoon oregano
- ¹/₂ teaspoon marjoram

¼ teaspoon thyme
½ teaspoon garlic powder
1 teaspoon sugar

1. In a medium covered saucepan, steam onion and bell pepper over low heat in ¼ cup of vegetable juice until soft.

2. Add remainder of the vegetable juice and all remaining ingredients. Simmer 20 to 25 minutes, uncovered, until sauce is reduced to 2 cups. Correct the seasonings.

Nutritional Data

PER SERVING		EXCHANGES	
Calories:	164	Milk:	0.0
% Calories from fat:	28	Vegetable:	1.7
Fat (gm):	5.1	Fruit:	0.0
Sat. fat (gm):	3.4	Bread:	0.3
Cholesterol (mg):	20.7	Meat:	1.1
Sodium (mg):	162	Fat:	0.4
Protein (gm):	9.2		
Carbohydrate (gm):	8.9		

BRANDIED LIVER PÂTÉ SHELLS

Guaranteed to make a liver-lover out of anyone! Souffle-like, sophisticated, and nutritionally superb, keep this power spread in the refrigerator for when you need extra stamina.

Serves 20 (2 shells each)

10 French, *or* sourdough, rolls
   Vegetable cooking spray
   Brandied Liver Spread (recipe follows)
1 medium tomato, seeded, finely chopped
1¼ cups nonfat sour cream
4 tablespoons finely chopped walnuts

1. Preheat oven to 400 degrees.

2. Cut a roll in half. Using fork, pull bread out of center, forming 2 shells, each about 1/4 in. thick. Spray insides of shells with nonstick cooking spray. Repeat with other rolls. Coat a baking sheet with nonstick spray. Set shells on sheet and bake 5 minutes or until golden and crisp.

3. Pat about 2 tablespoons of Brandied Liver Spread into each shell. Follow with a few chopped tomato pieces, 1 tablespoon of sour cream, and 1 teaspoon of chopped walnuts.

Brandied Liver Spread

3/4 lb. chicken livers
1 small onion, quartered
3/4 cup low-sodium beef broth
2 tablespoons Applejack brandy, *or* 2 teaspoons brandy extract
2 tablespoons frozen apple juice concentrate, thawed
1/2 teaspoon cardamom
1/2 teaspoon light salt
1 envelope plain gelatin
1 medium apple, peeled and chopped

1. Clean chicken livers, cut each in half, and remove connecting tissue. Combine livers, onion, and beef broth in a medium saucepan. Bring to boiling and cook 5 to 8 minutes, covered.

2. Empty mixture into blender container, including liquid. Add brandy, apple juice concentrate, cardamom, light salt, gelatin, and apple. Cover and mix on high speed until well blended.

3. Pour into a small crock or 3-cup mold and chill overnight.

Nutritional Data

PER SERVING		EXCHANGES	
Calories:	233	Milk:	0.0
% Calories from fat:	17	Vegetable:	0.2
Fat (gm):	4.5	Fruit:	1.0
Sat. fat (gm):	0.8	Bread:	0.0
Cholesterol (mg):	194.7	Meat:	0.8
Sodium (mg):	235	Fat:	0.0
Protein (gm):	12.4		
Carbohydrate (gm):	35.1		

LOBSTER TACOS

Serves 3

9 ozs. lobster, cooked (about 2 cups)
1/4 cup minced green onion
1/4 cup minced green bell pepper
Juice of 1 lime
2 tablespoons salsa, purchased
2 tablespoons chopped cilantro
1/2 teaspoon oregano
Hot pepper sauce, to taste
3 prepared taco shells
2 cups shredded lettuce
Bottled red, *or* green, chili sauce, optional

1. In a small bowl, flake lobster with a fork. Add onions, green pepper, lime juice, salsa, cilantro, oregano, and hot sauce. Mix well.
2. Pack taco shells with filling. Stuff shredded lettuce over filling and season with chili sauce, if desired.

Nutritional Data

PER SERVING		EXCHANGES	
Calories:	193	Milk:	0.0
% Calories from fat:	28	Vegetable:	0.3
Fat (gm):	6	Fruit:	0.0
Sat. fat (gm):	0.7	Bread:	0.7
Cholesterol (mg):	61.9	Meat:	2.1
Sodium (mg):	464	Fat:	0.7
Protein (gm):	18.8		
Carbohydrate (gm):	14.2		

CHICKEN PICADILLO TAMALES

Wrap this lean, spicy filling in corn husks.

Serves 12

12 dried corn husks, soaked in warm water 1 hour, drained, and dried (if not available, use 12, 10-in. squares of aluminum foil)
    Vegetable cooking spray
 2 large (6-oz.) cooked chicken breasts, shredded
3/4 cup chopped onion
 2 cloves garlic, minced
 2 cups chopped tomatoes, *or* 1, 16-oz. can no-salt-added chopped tomatoes, drained
 1 medium apple, chopped (1 cup)
1/4 cup golden raisins
 1 4-oz. can chopped green chilies
1/2 teaspoon crushed oregano leaves
1/4 teaspoon ground cumin
1/2 teaspoon cinnamon
 1 tablespoon vinegar
    Red pepper sauce, such as Tabasco, optional
    Nonfat sour cream, optional

1. Soak corn husks in warm water. Meanwhile . . .

2. Coat a 10-in. nonstick skillet with vegetable spray and bring to a medium-high heat. Saute chicken with onion and garlic 2 minutes, stirring to sear in flavor. Stir in remainder of ingredients(except red pepper sauce and sour cream) and cook 10 to 15 minutes or until apple is soft.

3. Spoon about 3 tablespoons of filling down center of each corn husk. Fold husk over, enclosing filling, then roll husk to form a round tamale. Fold up bottom of husk and tie both ends with strips of husk or string. (Tamales may be frozen at this point.)

4. Place tamales on a rack in a kettle or steamer and steam 10 minutes. (If using aluminum foil, prick holes in foil so filling will steam.) To serve, remove tamales from husks and pass red pepper sauce and non-fat sour cream, if desired.

Nutritional Data

PER SERVING		EXCHANGES	
Calories:	110	Milk:	0.0
% Calories from fat:	14	Vegetable:	0.3
Fat (gm):	1.8	Fruit:	0.8
Sat. fat (gm):	0.4	Bread:	0.0
Cholesterol (mg):	23.9	Meat:	1.3
Sodium (mg):	42	Fat:	0.0
Protein (gm):	9.9		
Carbohydrate (gm):	14.2		

TERIYAKI SWORDFISH SANDWICH

Sometimes referred to as "the steak of seafood," shark is enhanced by this delicious teriyaki marinade. Fresh tuna may be substituted.

Serves 4

Marinade (recipe follows)
4   4-oz. swordfish steaks
4   calorie-reduced hamburger buns, lightly toasted
4   tablespoons nonfat mayonnaise
4   lettuce leaves
    Alfalfa sprouts, for garnish

1. Place Marinade in heavy plastic bag along with swordfish steaks and refrigerate 1 to 2 hours, turning bag occasionally to marinate thoroughly all surfaces of the fish.

2. Remove swordfish from bag and grill over high heat 3 to 4 minutes on each side, turning once. Be careful not to overcook swordfish—it dries out quickly! Fish is done when flesh flakes easily with a fork.

3. Spread 1 tablespoon of mayonnaise over both sides of each bun and tuck swordfish steaks between. Serve with lettuce leaves and alfalfa sprouts on the side.

Marinade

¹/₂ cup light soy sauce
¹/₄ cup pineapple juice
¹/₄ cup dry sherry
  1 tablespoon brown sugar
¹/₂ teaspoon ground ginger
  1 clove garlic, pressed
  2 teaspoons lemon juice

1. In a nonreactive bowl, combine all ingredients.

Nutritional Data

PER SERVING		EXCHANGES	
Calories:	153	Milk:	0.0
% Calories from fat:	27	Vegetable:	0.0
Fat (gm):	4.5	Fruit:	0.0
Sat. fat (gm):	1.2	Bread:	0.2
Cholesterol (mg):	44	Meat:	3.1
Sodium (mg):	589	Fat:	0.0
Protein (gm):	22.7		
Carbohydrate (gm):	4.4		

POLISH KOLACHKY

Lighten up and simplify a Polish favorite. Canned refrigerator biscuits (just 50 calories and 1 gram of fat each) are filled with a sweet, nonfat cheese filling.

Serves 10

     Vegetable cooking spray
  1 cup nonfat cottage cheese
¹/₂ cup nonfat cream cheese
  2 tablespoons sugar
  3 tablespoons raisins
  1 teaspoon vanilla
  1 pkg. (7¹/₂ ozs., 10 biscuits) refrigerated biscuits
     Quick Icing (recipe follows)

1. Preheat oven to 425 degrees.

2. Coat baking pan with nonstick vegetable spray. Blend together cottage cheese, cream cheese, sugar, raisins, and vanilla.

3. Roll each biscuit into a ball, then form a rounded patty with the palm of your hand. Make a 1½ to 2-in. indentation with thumb in center of biscuit. Spoon about 2 tablespoons of filling into center of each biscuit, and place biscuits in pan, 1 in. apart.

4. Bake 10 to 13 minutes or until golden brown. Ice with Quick Icing (recipe follows) while still warm. Eat warm or cool.

Quick Icing

½ cup powdered sugar, sifted
2 teaspoons nonfat milk

1. Combine powdered sugar with milk, stirring until dissolved.

Nutritional Data

PER SERVING		EXCHANGES	
Calories:	102	Milk:	0.1
% Calories from fat:	9	Vegetable:	0.2
Fat (gm):	1	Fruit:	0.0
Sat. fat (gm):	Trace	Bread:	0.7
Cholesterol (mg):	2.5	Meat:	0.2
Sodium (mg):	279	Fat:	0.2
Protein (gm):	4.2		
Carbohydrate (gm):	19.7		

SCANDINAVIAN PICKLED FISH SANDWICH

Pickling is one of the most flavorful methods of preparing fish. Scandinavians traditionally marinate salmon and call it gravlax. Salmon is tasty and popular but high in fat. I prefer leaner fish such as snapper, sole, and cod.

Serves 4, generously

2 lbs. Marinated Fish Filets (recipe follows)
½ cup nonfat sour cream

1 medium apple, thinly sliced
$\frac{1}{2}$ small red onion, thinly sliced
  Salt and pepper, to taste
8 slices calorie-reduced whole-wheat bread
  Fresh dill, for garnish
  Watercress, for garnish

1. Remove fish from marinade and pat dry on paper towels. Cut in thin slivers. In a medium-size bowl, combine marinated fish, sour cream, apple, and onions. Season with salt and pepper and mix well.

2. Spread filling over four of the bread slices. Follow with sprigs of fresh dill and watercress; cover with remaining slices of bread. Cut crusts off sandwiches, if desired, and cut each in half diagonally.

Marinated Fish Filets
Marinating time: 2 days

1 tablespoon each: salt, sugar
$1\frac{1}{4}$ teaspoons dried dill weed
$\frac{1}{4}$ teaspoon freshly ground black pepper
2 lbs. low-fat fish filets, such as red snapper, halibut, haddock, sole, flounder, cod, or hake (or coho salmon, optional)
1 cup red wine vinegar

1. With a mortar and pestle, thoroughly crush together salt, sugar, dill weed, and pepper. Sprinkle half of this mixture in bottom of a glass dish just large enough to hold the fish.

2. Place fish in dish and rub remaining mixture into fish. Pour vinegar over fish and cover tightly with plastic wrap or aluminum foil.

3. Refrigerate for at least 2 days, spooning juices over fish at least 4 times a day.

Nutritional Data (using Halibut)

PER SERVING		EXCHANGES	
Calories:	250	Milk:	0.2
% Calories from fat:	14	Vegetable:	0.4
Fat (gm):	3.8	Fruit:	0.0
Sat. fat (gm):	0.6	Bread:	1.4
Cholesterol (mg):	36	Meat:	2.8
Sodium (mg):	290	Fat:	0.2
Protein (gm):	29		
Carbohydrate (gm):	25.6		

Nutritional Data *(using Coho Salmon)*

PER SERVING		EXCHANGES	
Calories:	337	Milk:	0.2
% Calories from fat:	36	Vegetable:	0.4
Fat (gm):	13.5	Fruit:	0.0
Sat. fat (gm):	2.7	Bread:	1.4
Cholesterol (mg):	66	Meat:	3.2
Sodium (mg):	296	Fat:	1.0
Protein (gm):	29.1		
Carbohydrate (gm):	26.8		

BEEF ROLL-UPS

Serves 4

1 10-oz. pkg. frozen mixed vegetables, thawed
¼ cup nonfat sour cream
2 tablespoons minced parsley
1 teaspoon lemon juice
½ teaspoon dried tarragon, crushed
4 ozs. deli sliced lean roast beef
4 flour tortillas (8 in.)
   Alfalfa sprouts, for garnish

1. Cook vegetables according to package directions; drain. Add sour cream, minced parsley, lemon juice, and tarragon and mix well.

2. Position tortilla on a 12-in. sheet of plastic wrap. Spread ⅔ cup vegetable mixture to within ½ in. of edges. Cover with roast beef slice and alfalfa sprouts. Roll up. Repeat with remaining tortillas.

3. Wrap roll-ups tightly with plastic wrap. Refrigerate 2 hours or overnight to blend flavors. To serve, unwrap and cut rolls in half.

Nutritional Data

PER SERVING		EXCHANGES	
Calories:	189	Milk:	0.1
% Calories from fat:	15	Vegetable:	0.8
Fat (gm):	3.2	Fruit:	0.0
Sat. fat (gm):	0.6	Bread:	1.6
Cholesterol (mg):	15	Meat:	0.5
Sodium (mg):	490	Fat:	0.5
Protein (gm):	11.1		
Carbohydrate (gm):	28.9		

CURRIED TURKEY PITA PATTIES

Serves 6

1 lb. lean ground turkey breast
1 cup finely chopped onion
1 egg white, beaten
2 teaspoons each: ground cumin and curry powder
3 pita breads, cut in half
Slices of onion and tomato, for garnish
3/4 cup plain low-fat yogurt
2 tablespoons minced fresh cilantro leaves

1. Combine turkey, onions, egg white, cumin, and curry powder and mix lightly. Shape into 6 flat patties.

2. Pan fry in a nonstick skillet 2 to 3 minutes on each side until done. Drain away any fat and pat dry on paper towels.

3. Open pita breads to form pockets; add hot turkey patties and complete with onion and tomato slices, yogurt, and minced cilantro.

Nutritional Data

PER SERVING		EXCHANGES	
Calories:	228	Milk:	0.2
% Calories from fat:	26	Vegetable:	0.3
Fat (gm):	6.5	Fruit:	0.0
Sat. fat (gm):	1.7	Bread:	1.1
Cholesterol (mg):	60	Meat:	2.0
Sodium (mg):	269	Fat:	0.2
Protein (gm):	18.9		
Carbohydrate (gm):	22		

Sweet & Sour Turkey Barbecue

Serves 4

Vegetable cooking spray
2 large cloves garlic, crushed
1 cup finely chopped onion
½ green bell pepper, chopped
2 stalks celery, chopped
1 teaspoon finely chopped fresh ginger, *or*
¾ teaspoon powdered ginger
¾ teaspoon cayenne pepper
¾ cup crushed pineapple in juice
1 cup peeled, chopped tomato
2 tablespoons sugar
2 tablespoons cider vinegar
2 tablespoons Dijon-style mustard
2 cups dice, cooked white turkey meat
4 calorie-reduced hamburger buns

1. In medium skillet coated with nonstick spray, saute garlic, onions, bell pepper, and celery over medium-low heat. Cook about 5 minutes or until soft. Stir in ginger and cayenne.

2. Drain juice from the pineapple and pour juice into skillet. Bring to a boil over medium-high heat. Add crushed pineapple, tomato, sugar, vinegar, and mustard. Combine well, then stir in turkey. Simmer, covered, for 10 minutes.

3. Serve over split hamburger buns.

Nutritional Data

PER SERVING		EXCHANGES	
Calories:	164	Milk:	0.0
% Calories from fat:	12	Vegetable:	1.3
Fat (gm):	2.2	Fruit:	0.5
Sat. fat (gm):	Trace	Bread:	0.9
Cholesterol (mg):	5.9	Meat:	0.3
Sodium (mg):	395	Fat:	0.2
Protein (gm):	8		
Carbohydrate (gm):	28.3		

OYSTER "LOAVES"

The oyster loaf was the granddaddy of the New Orleans Poor Boy Sandwich. Called the "peacemaker," many a New Orleans husband would bring one home to placate an angry wife, certain that such treatment would settle any quarrel. The classic New Orleans oyster loaf consists of a loaf of fresh French bread sliced in half across and then in half lengthwise, warmed in the oven, then buttered and filled with freshly fried oysters. This version is light and lean because the oysters are baked in a spicy, crunchy coating and stuffed into a sourdough roll. Increase the recipe if you like, to make a meal out of a hollowed-out loaf of bread!

Serves 3

- 1 egg white
- 3/4 teaspoon blackening seasoning, *or* 1/4 teaspoon each: dried thyme, oregano, and basil plus 1/8 teaspoon cayenne pepper
- 2 slices crispbread, *or* day-old bread, crushed
- 1 8-oz. can oysters, drained (about 12)
  Vegetable cooking spray
- 3 French sourdough rolls (3 in.)
- 3 tablespoons nonfat mayonnaise
- 1 1/2 cups finely shredded lettuce
- 1 large tomato, cut into 1/4-in.-thick slices

1. Preheat oven to 400 degrees.

2. In a clean, medium-sized metal or glass bowl, beat egg white until fairly stiff, about 2 minutes.

3. In another bowl, combine seasonings with crumbs and toss well to combine. Put mixture in plastic bag.

4. Using your hands, dip oysters, one by one, into the stiff egg white then toss into the bag filled with the crumb mixture. Shake until coated. Coat a pie plate with nonstick spray. Place oysters in pan, and bake 10 to 15 minutes or until oysters are crunchy.

5. Cut tops from rolls. Using a fork, then your fingers, hollow out rolls, leaving the crusty shell as thin as possible. Spray these bread "boats" with nonstick spray. Place the shells on a baking sheet and bake in middle of oven 10 minutes or until crisp and golden brown.

6. To assemble oyster "loaves," spread 1 tablespoon mayonnaise inside each shell. Scatter shredded lettuce in bottom, and arrange tomato slices, and, finally, oysters over it. Gently squeeze tops, back onto rolls and serve.

Nutritional Data

PER SERVING		EXCHANGES	
Calories:	202	Milk:	0.0
% Calories from fat:	17	Vegetable:	0.2
Fat (gm):	3.7	Fruit:	0.0
Sat. fat (gm):	0.9	Bread:	1.7
Cholesterol (mg):	45	Meat:	1.0
Sodium (mg):	548	Fat:	0.3
Protein (gm):	11.3		
Carbohydrate (gm):	29.8		

CREOLE BEAN BROIL

Serves 2

- ⅓ cup finely chopped green bell pepper
- ¼ cup finely chopped onion
- 1 cup red beans
- ¼ cup chopped tomatoes
- 3–5 drops liquid smoke
- ¼ teaspoon dried oregano, crushed
- ¼ teaspoon dried thyme, crushed
- ⅛ teaspoon garlic powder
- ¼ teaspoon sweet paprika
- 2 ozs. lean ham, diced
- 2 calorie-reduced hamburger buns
- 2 slices nonfat processed Cheddar cheese
  Chopped fresh parsley, for garnish

1. In a microwave-safe bowl, combine green pepper, onions, beans, tomatoes, liquid smoke, all herbs, and ham. Microwave (high) 2 to 3 minutes.

2. Place buns on microwave-safe plate. Pour half of filling over each bun. Cover with cheese slice.

3. Return buns to microwave. Cook (medium) 30 seconds or until cheese melts. Sprinkle with chopped parsley. Serve immediately.

Nutritional Data

PER SERVING		EXCHANGES	
Calories:	249	Milk:	0.2
% Calories from fat:	10	Vegetable:	0.8
Fat (gm):	2.6	Fruit:	0.0
Sat. fat (gm):	0.3	Bread:	2.2
Cholesterol (mg):	15	Meat:	1.5
Sodium (mg):	631	Fat:	0.5
Protein (gm):	18.5		
Carbohydrate (gm):	36.8		

VEGETARIAN TEA SANDWICHES

Fresh herbs adhere magically to the edges of these dainty, round sandwiches.

Serves 1

4 slices calorie-reduced white, *or* wheat, bread
    2½-in. biscuit cutter
¼ teaspoon seasoning salt *or* to taste
2 paper-thin onion slices, each about 2½ in. diameter
2 thin tomato slices, each about 2½ in. diameter
3 tablespoons nonfat sour cream, *or* mayonnaise
¼ cup each, very finely chopped fresh: parsley, cilantro, dill, or any combination of these

1. With biscuit cutter, cut a round from each slice of bread.

2. Sprinkle each side of bread rounds with seasoning salt. Place an onion and tomato slice on bread rounds, then top other 2 bread rounds.

3. Place sour cream and fresh herbs each in separate shallow bowls. Dip sandwich edges in sour cream, then into fresh herbs, making sure there are no bare spots. Chill well before serving.

Nutritional Data

PER SERVING		EXCHANGES	
Calories:	179	Milk:	0.1
% Calories from fat:	10	Vegetable:	0.3
Fat (gm):	1.9	Fruit:	0.0
Sat. fat (gm):	0.4	Bread:	2.3
Cholesterol (mg):	0	Meat:	0.0
Sodium (mg):	686	Fat:	0.3
Protein (gm):	8.3		
Carbohydrate (gm):	37.5		

NEW ORLEANS HOT DOG

A complete meal in a bun!

Serves 1

1　low-fat hot dog
1　calorie-reduced hot dog bun
½　cup Creole Chili (recipe follows)

1. Cook hot dog per package directions. Toast bun under broiler until toasted, 2 to 3 minutes. (Or warm bun in microwave by wrapping in paper towel and cooking (medium) 5 seconds or just until warm.)

2. Tuck hot dog into bun and spoon Creole Chili over it. Serve nice and hot!

Nutritional Data *(not including Creole Chili)*

PER SERVING		EXCHANGES	
Calories:	179	Milk:	0.0
% Calories from fat:	15	Vegetable:	1.6
Fat (gm):	3.1	Fruit:	0.0
Sat. fat (gm):	0.5	Bread:	1.0
Cholesterol (mg):	15	Meat:	0.2
Sodium (mg):	680	Fat:	0.0
Protein (gm):	11.4		
Carbohydrate (gm):	26.7		

Creole Chili
Makes 2 cups

3/4 cup low-sodium beef stock, *or* bouillon
1/2 cup chopped onion
1/2 cup chopped green bell pepper
1/2 cup chopped celery
2 teaspoons chili powder
1/3 cup tomato sauce
1 medium clove garlic, crushed
2 teaspoons Worcestershire sauce
1 teaspoon brown sugar
2 teaspoons cider vinegar

1. In a medium saucepan, bring beef stock to a boil. Add onions, green pepper, and celery. Simmer, covered, over low heat 5 minutes. Add remaining ingredients; stir and simmer, uncovered, 10 minutes more.

Nutritional Data

PER 1/2-CUP SERVING		EXCHANGES	
Calories:	48	Milk:	0.0
% Calories from fat:	1	Vegetable:	1.6
Fat (gm):	0	Fruit:	0.0
Sat. fat (gm):	0	Bread:	0.1
Cholesterol (mg):	0	Meat:	0.0
Sodium (mg):	116	Fat:	0.0
Protein (gm):	1.4		
Carbohydrate (gm):	11.3		

VIETNAMESE SPRING ROLLS

Vietnamese rice papers are tissue thin, brittle, and imprinted with an intricate crosshatch pattern that comes from the bamboo mats on which they have been laid out to dry. Rice paper should be softened before using. (See "How to Prepare Rice Paper" below.) It is then ready to eat and can be used, burrito-like, to wrap a multitude of fillings such as cooked meat, vegetables, or even fruit. Once you've mastered the technique, don't be surprised if you find yourself wrapping up every leftover in the refrigerator, like I did. Eat rice paper raw, baked or deep-fried. Rice paper requires no refrigeration and will last for months if kept protected from breakage and moisture. Assemble these rolls ahead of time and serve as appetizers. Or omit the rice paper and simply wrap filling in lettuce leaves.

Serves 4 (2 rolls each)

1 cup thin rice noodles, soaked
8 rice paper circles, each 8½ in. diameter
4 large Boston lettuce leaves, ribs removed and discarded, leaves halved lengthwise
8 ozs. cooked chicken breast, sliced into 2 x 2 x ½-in. strips
1 medium carrot, shredded
½ cup fresh mung beansprouts
½ cup mint leaves
8 cooked medium shrimp, peeled, deveined, and halved lengthwise
½ cup fresh cilantro leaves
Sweet-and-Sour Dipping Sauce (recipe follows)

1. Soak rice noodles in 2 cups warm water until softened. Drain well and set aside.

2. Center half a lettuce leaf at bottom of 1 rice paper, leaving a 2-in. border of paper around bottom edge. Place rice noodles on bottom half of lettuce leaf. Sprinkle noodles with 1 oz. chicken, 1 tablespoon shredded carrot, and a sprinkling of beansprouts and mint leaves.

3. Lift edge of rice paper and carefully fold it over filling. Make first roll as tight and firm as possible, but be careful to prevent tearing. Roll spring roll over once, and then fold sides over so that roll is closed at both ends. Continue to roll until spring roll is almost rolled up.

4. Place 2 shrimp halves, cut side down, on top of the rice-paper-enclosed filling, Finish rolling the last turn of the rice paper over shrimp.

5. Transfer roll, seam side down, to a platter; cover with damp paper towel. Repeat for remaining rolls. Serve with cilantro garnish and Sweet-and-Sour Dipping Sauce, or seasoned rice vinegar.

How to Prepare Rice Paper: Spread an absorbent, damp towel on your work surface. Fill a large pan with lukewarm water. Preparing 1 paper at a time, completely immerse a sheet of rice paper in water. Let it soak, 2 to 3 seconds or until *barely* soft. Immediately transfer rice paper from water to damp towel.

Nutritional Data *(not including Sweet-and-Sour Dipping Sauce)*

PER SERVING		EXCHANGES	
Calories:	65	Milk:	0.0
% Calories from fat:	25	Vegetable:	0.2
Fat (gm):	1.7	Fruit:	0.0
Sat. fat (gm):	0.3	Bread:	0.6
Cholesterol (mg):	51.5	Meat:	1.7
Sodium (mg):	115	Fat:	0.4
Protein (gm):	6.9		
Carbohydrate (gm):	5.7		

Sweet-and-Sour Dipping Sauce
Makes 1¼ cups

½ cup seasoned rice vinegar
½ cup rice vinegar
¼ cup low-sodium ketchup
2 teaspoons red chili sauce*
½ cup water

1. Combine ingredients and stir until well blended.

*Available in oriental groceries or specialty food section of your grocery store.

Nutritional Data

PER 1 TABLESPOON SERVING

		EXCHANGES	
Calories:	8.6	Milk:	0.0
% Calories from fat:	1	Vegetable:	0.2
Fat (gm):	Trace	Fruit:	0.0
Sat. fat (gm):	0	Bread:	0.0
Cholesterol (mg):	0	Meat:	0.0
Sodium (mg):	80	Fat:	0.0
Protein (gm):	0		
Carbohydrate (gm):	1.8		

APPLE CHEDDAR SPRING ROLLS

Another rice paper sandwich. Rice paper can be purchased in oriental markets.

Serves 3

1 large Pippin apple, unpeeled, cored, and finely chopped (1½ cups)
2 teaspoons lime juice
1 packet artificial sweetener (not containing aspartame), *or* 2 teaspoons sugar
1 teaspoon mace
1 tablespoon fresh mint leaves, *or* 1 teaspoon dried, crushed
4 ozs. nonfat sharp Cheddar cheese, shredded
2 tablespoons finely chopped walnuts
3 rice paper circles, each 8½ in.
  Butter-flavored vegetable cooking spray
  Nonfat vanilla yogurt, optional

1. In a medium bowl, toss together chopped apple, lime juice, artificial sweetener (or sugar), mace, mint leaves, Cheddar cheese, and walnuts.

2. Prepare rice paper according to instructions in previous recipe.

3. Place approximately ³/₄ cup of the filling on rice paper, midway between center and edge nearest you, leaving a 2-in. border of rice paper around side edges. Roll once, the close roll by folding paper in from the sides: then roll up tightly. Spray with vegetable spray to keep from drying out. Repeat for remaining rolls.

4. Bake in 375-degree preheated oven until rolls are crisp and golden brown, about 20 minutes. Serve cold with vanilla yogurt, if desired.

Nutritional Data

PER SERVING		EXCHANGES	
Calories:	243	Milk:	0.1
% Calories from fat:	16	Vegetable:	0.0
Fat (gm):	4.4	Fruit:	2.3
Sat. fat (gm):	0.6	Bread:	0.0
Cholesterol (mg):	6.7	Meat:	1.8
Sodium (mg):	314	Fat:	0.6
Protein (gm):	14.9		
Carbohydrate (gm):	40.7		

RATATOUILLE BUNS WITH SAUSAGE

A "European" sloppy Joe.

Serves 6

¹/₂ medium eggplant
3 medium zucchini, sliced
1 green bell pepper, chopped
2 cups chopped onions
2 large tomatoes, cut into chunks
1 clove garlic, minced
¹/₂ cup minced parsley
2 teaspoons crushed oregano
1 teaspoon crushed basil
¹/₂ teaspoon thyme

³/₄ lb. Low-Fat Italian Sausage (recipe follows),
        cut into ¹/₂-in. slices
6 calorie-reduced hamburger buns

1. Peel and cut eggplant into ¹/₂-in. cubes. Place in colander. Shake salt over eggplant and allow to sit for an hour or so. Rinse off salt under running water.

2. Combine all ingredients, except sausage and buns, in a 4-quart casserole. Bake, covered, at 350 degrees 1 hour, then ¹/₂ hour, uncovered. Or, cover with plastic wrap and microwave (high) 8 to 10 minutes or until tender. Stir occasionally to distribute juices.

3. Serve hot over split buns with sausage.

Low-Fat Italian Sausage
Makes ³/₄ lb.

³/₄ lb. ground turkey breast
2 teaspoons garlic powder
1 teaspoon red pepper flakes
¹/₂ teaspoon cayenne pepper
¹/₂ teaspoon coarse black pepper
³/₄ teaspoon light salt
1 teaspoon fennel seeds
1 teaspoon Italian seasoning blend
¹/₄ cup dry red wine
1 teaspoon sugar

1. Combine all ingredients in a medium bowl and lightly knead with bare hands.

2. Place approximately ¹/₃ cup of sausage mixture into center of a piece of plastic wrap, and roll firmly into a log shape. Twist ends of plastic wrap and tie with string. Cut off excess plastic. Repeat, using remaining sausage.

3. Poach sausages in simmering water 10 minutes. Unwrap plastic and serve immediately or refrigerate.

Nutritional Data

PER SERVING		EXCHANGES	
Calories:	249	Milk:	0.0
% Calories from fat:	28	Vegetable:	1.0
Fat (gm):	7.8	Fruit:	0.0
Sat. fat (gm):	1.6	Bread:	1.2
Cholesterol (mg):	59.8	Meat:	1.9
Sodium (mg):	455	Fat:	0.3
Protein (gm):	18.9		
Carbohydrate (gm):	23.2		

Miniature Hoagie "Au Jus"

Serves 1

1 calorie-reduced hot dog bun
2 teaspoons mustard
1 tablespoon ketchup
2½ oz. deli lean-sliced turkey, or chicken, or beef
3 tomato slices
2 red onion slices
1 curly lettuce leaf
1 small dill pickle, sliced
½ cup French Onion Sauce (recipe follows)

1. Spread bun generously with mustard and ketchup.
2. Layer meat, tomato, onion, lettuce, and pickle into bun. Close and slice in half with diagonal cut. Serve with French Onion Sauce in small bowl on the side. Dip sandwich into sauce as you eat it.

Variation: Substitute barbecue sauce for French Onion Sauce.

Nutritional Data *(not including French Onion Sauce)*

PER SERVING		EXCHANGES	
Calories:	201	Milk:	0.0
% Calories from fat:	17	Vegetable:	0.2
Fat (gm):	3.7	Fruit:	0.0
Sat. fat (gm):	0.5	Bread:	1.2
Cholesterol (mg):	25	Meat:	1.5
Sodium (mg):	845	Fat:	0.7
Protein (gm):	17.6		
Carbohydrate (gm):	24.6		

French Onion Sauce

Makes 5½ cups

Vegetable cooking spray
3 cups sliced onions
6 cups low-sodium beef broth

1. Coat skillet with cooking spray. Saute onions over medium heat until transparent. Combine with beef broth in a small stockpot. Cover tightly and simmer 1 hour. Store excess in refrigerator for up to 1 week.

Nutritional Data

PER ½-CUP SERVING		EXCHANGES	
Calories:	31	Milk:	0.0
% Calories from fat:	0	Vegetable:	0.7
Fat (gm):	0	Fruit:	0.0
Sat. fat (gm):	0	Bread:	0.0
Cholesterol (mg):	0	Meat:	0.4
Sodium (mg):	47	Fat:	0.0
Protein (gm):	3.3		
Carbohydrate (gm):	4.5		

TANDOORI TUNA ROLLS

Tandoori paste is an Indian seasoning and marinade that can be found in the international foods section of larger supermarkets. (Patak brand is excellent.) Or make your own with the recipe below. This spicy orange paste makes a brightly aromatic marinade for chicken, as well.

Serves 2 (2 rolls each)

1 6¾-oz. can tuna in water, drained
¾ cup celery
⅓ cup finely chopped onion
½ cup Tandoori Paste (recipe follows)
2 12 x 17-in. sheets phyllo dough
Vegetable cooking spray

1. Preheat oven to 375 degrees. In a small bowl, combine tuna, celery, and onions. Prepare Tandoori paste (or use commercial). Mix with tuna and vegetables.

2. Unroll phyllo dough. Remove 2 sheets to working surface. Wrap remaining phyllo dough in plastic wrap and return to refrigerator.

3. Cut sheet in half. Spray surface of dough with vegetable spray. Spoon 3 tablespoons of filling onto lower edge of rectangle and roll up, tucking in final corner with your finger. Repeat with remaining 3 sheets.

4. Bake in preheated oven 10 to 15 minutes or until light brown and crispy.

Tandoori Paste
Makes ½ cup

- 2 teaspoons curry powder
- ½ teaspoon cumin
- ½ teaspoon powdered ginger
- ⅛ teaspoon powdered garlic, optional
- ½ cup nonfat yogurt

1. Combine all ingredients in a small bowl.

Nutritional Data

PER SERVING		EXCHANGES	
Calories:	214	Milk:	0.4
% Calories from fat:	8	Vegetable:	0.0
Fat (gm):	1.9	Fruit:	0.0
Sat. fat (gm):	0.3	Bread:	0.7
Cholesterol (mg):	29	Meat:	3.4
Sodium (mg):	473	Fat:	0.2
Protein (gm):	29.7		
Carbohydrate (gm):	17.7		

BLACKENED FISH SANDWICH

Chef Paul Prudhomme invented the "blackening" cooking method. Paul experimented by laying fish directly in the fire, which seared and blackened it, greatly intensifying the flavor. When he first moved to his restaurant in New Orleans, he used a black cast-iron skillet on the stove because he couldn't afford a stove hood: blackened fish was born! This Blackening Seasoning recipe is a reduced sodium version of his product, which is commercially available. Reserve any remaining seasoning to blacken more fish, steak, turkey, and chicken cutlets—even alligator! Hot dog buns are naturally shaped to enclose fish filets.

Serves 2

Blackening Seasoning (recipe follows), or purchase

- 2 5-oz. white fish filets (cod, halibut, perch, orange roughy, catfish, pike or red snapper)

　　1　egg white, beaten until frothy
　　2　calorie-reduced hot dog buns
　　4　tablespoons Citrus Tartar Sauce (see p. 160) *or*
　　　　Creole mustard, commercially available, both
　　　　optional
　　1　tomato, sliced
　　　　Curly lettuce leaves, for garnish

1.　Turn on the kitchen fan, or use your barbecue grill outdoors. Place a cast-iron skillet over high heat until it smokes, about 10 minutes.

2.　Transfer about 1 tablespoon Blackening Seasoning into a shallow bowl or onto a sheet of waxed paper, reserving the rest for future use.

3.　Dip fish filets into egg white so that both sides are coated. Drag fish through seasoning mix and pat more seasoning over fish to ensure complete coverage. Carefully drop filets into sizzling hot, dry skillet. (Do not add butter or oil.) Cook, uncovered, over high heat until underside looks good and black, 1 to 2 minutes. Turn and cook other side 1 minute or until blackened. Remove filets.

4.　Toast inside of buns in the same pan 1 minute or until golden brown. If desired, spread with Citrus Tartar Sauce (Chapter 6) or Creole mustard.

5.　Place filets in buns and cover with tomato slices and lettuce.

Note: Serve with hush puppies, coleslaw, greens, light beer, and some good Cajun music.

Blackening Seasoning
　　1　tablespoon sweet paprika
　　1　teaspoon salt, optional
　　1　teaspoon onion powder
　　1　teaspoon garlic powder
　　1　teaspoon ground cayenne pepper
　3/4　teaspoon white pepper
　3/4　teaspoon black pepper
　1/2　teaspoon dried thyme leaves
　1/2　teaspoon dried oregano leaves

1.　Combine all ingredients in a small jar.

Nutritional Data

PER SERVING		EXCHANGES	
Calories:	232	Milk:	0.0
% Calories from fat:	11	Vegetable:	0.2
Fat (gm):	2.6	Fruit:	0.0
Sat. fat (gm):	0.2	Bread:	0.9
Cholesterol (mg):	80	Meat:	3.7
Sodium (mg):	330	Fat:	0.2
Protein (gm):	33.7		
Carbohydrate (gm):	18.5		

GRILLED PEANUT BUTTER AND BANANA SANDWICH

Serves 1

1 tablespoon reduced-fat chunky peanut butter
1 tablespoon nonfat cream cheese
2 slices reduced-calorie whole-wheat bread
1 tablespoon no-sugar-added strawberry jam
1/3 medium banana, sliced very thin
Butter-flavored vegetable cooking spray

1. In a small mixing bowl, combine peanut butter and cream cheese.

2. Spread peanut butter mixture on 1 slice of bread. Coat other slice with strawberry jam. Arrange slices of banana over jam and cover with first slice of bread. Spray sandwich with vegetable spray.

3. Coat a 10-in. nonstick skillet with vegetable spray. Cook sandwich over low-medium heat until bottom is lightly brown, pressing sandwich occasionally with spatula. Flip and grill other side, spraying again with vegetable spray. Cook 4 to 5 minutes more or until done. Cut in half diagonally and serve warm.

Nutritional Data

PER SERVING		EXCHANGES	
Calories:	250	Milk:	0.1
% Calories from fat:	26	Vegetable:	0.0
Fat (gm):	7.3	Fruit:	1.0
Sat. fat (gm):	1.3	Bread:	2.4
Cholesterol (mg):	2.5	Meat:	0.0
Sodium (mg):	368	Fat:	1.4
Protein (gm):	10.4		
Carbohydrate (gm):	40.4		

MUSHROOM, SAUSAGE & KRAUT BISCUITS

My sister Carol won $10,000 in the Pillsbury Bakeoff with a version of this recipe. She uses hot roll mix, but I prefer refrigerator biscuits.

Serves 10

1 8-oz. can sauerkraut, drained and rinsed well
1 cup chopped onion
3½ cups chopped fresh mushrooms
2½ tablespoons brown sugar
6 ozs. smoked turkey sausage, chopped, *or* low-fat smoked sausage, chopped
¼ cup light beer
Black pepper to taste
2 pkgs. (20 biscuits) refrigerator biscuits

1. Preheat oven to 425 degrees
2. Combine sauerkraut, onions, mushrooms, brown sugar, turkey sausage, and beer in a 1-quart saucepan. Cook over medium-low heat until sausage is cooked and mushrooms and onions are translucent, 15 to 20 minutes. Season with pepper to taste.
3. Press 2 refrigerator biscuits together. Place a piece of 12 x 12-in. waxed paper on the counter. Sprinkle waxed paper with flour, then

place biscuits on waxed paper. Sprinkle on a bit more flour, and top biscuits with second piece of waxed paper. Roll out into an 8-in. circle. Measure a heaping ¼ cup of filling into center of dough. Bring up edges toward center and pinch closed. Repeat with remaining biscuits.

4. Bake until light brown, 20 to 25 minutes. Delicious served warm.

Nutritional Data

PER SERVING		EXCHANGES	
Calories:	148	Milk:	0.0
% Calories from fat:	21	Vegetable:	0.6
Fat (gm):	3.6	Fruit:	0.0
Sat. fat (gm):	0.4	Bread:	1.5
Cholesterol (mg):	12	Meat:	0.3
Sodium (mg):	557	Fat:	0.7
Protein (gm):	5.6		
Carbohydrate (gm):	25.3		

FRUIT, WINE, AND CHEESE SOUFFLE SANDWICH

These can be assembled and ready to bake the day before.

Serves 1

Vegetable cooking spray
2 slices white, *or* wheat, reduced-calorie bread
¾ oz. low-fat Swiss cheese, shredded
¼ cup raw sweet cherries, pitted and chopped, *or*
  1 tablespoon no-sugar-added cherry preserves
¼ cup egg substitute
¼ cup evaporated skimmed milk
3 tablespoons dry white wine, *or* champagne
1 egg white

1. Preheat oven to 375 degrees.

2. Spray a ¾-cup casserole with nonstick cooking spray and place 1 slice of bread in casserole. Sprinkle with Swiss cheese, then top with chopped cherries (or preserves) and remaining bread slice.

3. Beat together egg substitute, milk, wine, and egg white, using a wire whisk. Pour egg substitute mixture over sandwich.

4. Bake 25 minutes or until a knife inserted in center comes out dry. Serve immediately.

Variation: Substitute raw mushrooms for cherries, and spread Dijon-style mustard on inside of top slice of bread.

Nutritional Data

PER SERVING		EXCHANGES	
Calories:	231	Milk:	0.7
% Calories from fat:	5	Vegetable:	0.0
Fat (gm):	1.3	Fruit:	0.5
Sat. fat (gm):	0.3	Bread:	1.4
Cholesterol (mg):	5.7	Meat:	1.7
Sodium (mg):	514	Fat:	0.2
Protein (gm):	20.7		
Carbohydrate (gm):	34.5		

HOT & SMOKY BLACK BEAN BURRITOS

Serves 6

1 15-oz. can black beans, drained
1 tablespoon chili powder
1/2 teaspoon garlic powder
1/2 teaspoon liquid smoke
1/2 cup frozen whole-kernel corn, thawed
6 flour tortillas (7-in.)
  Vegetable cooking spray
1 cup finely chopped onion
1/2 cup thinly sliced green bell pepper rings
1/2 cup thinly sliced red bell pepper rings
1/3 cup salsa, purchased
1 14 1/2-oz. can no-salt-added whole tomatoes, drained and chopped

1. Drain beans, reserving ¼ cup of liquid. Combine beans, reserved bean liquid, chili powder, garlic powder, and liquid smoke in food processor. Process until smooth. Spoon bean mixture into a bowl; stir in corn. Set aside.

2. Stack tortillas and wrap in damp paper towels. Microwave (high) 20 seconds. Spread ¼ cup bean mixture down center of each tortilla; roll up.

3. Place tortillas seam side down, in an 8-in.-square baking dish coated with cooking spray. Cover and bake at 350 degrees 30 minutes or until heated through. Set aside and cover with towel to keep warm.

4. Coat a nonstick skillet with cooking spray; place over medium-high heat until hot. Add onions and peppers; saute 5 minutes or until crisp-tender. Reduce heat to medium. Add salsa and tomatoes; simmer 1 minute. Serve over burritos.

Nutritional Data

PER SERVING		EXCHANGES	
Calories:	242	Milk:	0.0
% Calories from fat:	11	Vegetable:	1.4
Fat (gm):	3.1	Fruit:	0.0
Sat. fat (gm):	0.5	Bread:	2.4
Cholesterol (mg):	0.3	Meat:	0.0
Sodium (mg):	279	Fat:	0.5
Protein (gm):	9.9		
Carbohydrate (gm):	44.8		

6.
LIGHT SPREADS, CONDIMENTS & SAUCES

Commercial spreads and condiments—even the light varieties— are often excessive in fat, sodium, and sugar. So choose a better quality fuel for your body and whip up some homemade flavor enhancers (many take only a few minutes). Do it to cater to your personal taste preferences. Do it for the quality you get from fresh ingredients. Or just do it for the fun of it and the knowledge of what goes into the recipes.

CHOCOLATE CREAM CHEESE

Serves 8 (2 tablespoons each)

8 oz. nonfat cream cheese
3 tablespoons unsweetened cocoa powder
3 tablespoons sugar
1 teaspoon vanilla
½ teaspoon almond extract

1. Using an electric mixer, whip cream cheese, then add remaining ingredients and whip until completely blended. (A wooden spoon also works well.)

Variations: For Rum Raisin Cream Cheese, whip cream cheese with 2 tablespoons rum, ¼ cup raisins, and ¼ cup brown sugar.

Nutritional Data

PER SERVING		EXCHANGES	
Calories:	21	Milk:	0.1
% Calories from fat:	10	Vegetable:	0.0
Fat (gm):	0.2	Fruit:	0.0
Sat. fat (gm):	0	Bread:	0.0
Cholesterol (mg):	2.5	Meat:	0.0
Sodium (mg):	85	Fat:	0.0
Protein (gm):	2.1		
Carbohydrate (gm):	2.1		

STRAWBERRY PANCAKE SYRUP

This chameleon syrup is strawberry jelly when cold (great as topping for toast, bagels, or waffles), or warm it up in the microwave and poof! it's a syrup that's heartwarming over pancakes or ice milk.

Makes 3 cups

1½ cups water, divided
1 3-oz. pkg. sugar-free, strawberry-flavored gelatin
1 16-oz. pkg. unsweetened frozen whole straw-berries
1½ tablespoons cornstarch

1. Bring 1 cup water to a boil in a large saucepan. Add gelatin and stir well. Add strawberries and cook over medium-high heat for 5 minutes.

2. Combine cornstarch and ½ cup water; stir well and add to strawberry mixture. Bring to a boil and cook 1 minute, stirring constantly.

3. Place 1½ cups of mixture into container of an electric blender; cover and process until smooth. Pour syrup into a bowl; stir in remaining strawberry mixture. Serve warm or cold.

Nutritional Data

PER ¼-CUP SERVING		EXCHANGES	
Calories:	16	Milk:	0.0
% Calories from fat:	0	Vegetable:	0.0
Fat (gm):	0	Fruit:	0.1
Sat. fat (gm):	0	Bread:	0.1
Cholesterol (mg):	0	Meat:	0.0
Sodium (mg):	28	Fat:	0.0
Protein (gm):	0.3		
Carbohydrate (gm):	2.5		

JAMAICAN JERK SAUCE

Tangy, light, and refreshing on barbecued meats, vegetables, even poached eggs and omelets.

Makes 1¼ cups

2 cups low-salt vegetable cocktail
⅓ cup orange juice
1 teaspoon onion powder
½ cup white wine vinegar
1 teaspoon Worcestershire sauce
2 teaspoons brown sugar
¼ teaspoon ground cloves

1. In a 2-qt. saucepan, combine ingredients and simmer, uncovered, over low heat 10 to 15 minutes or until reduced in volume by approximately half.

Nutritional Data

PER 1-TABLESPOON SERVING		EXCHANGES	
		Milk:	0.0
Calories:	10	Vegetable:	0.2
% Calories from fat:	0	Fruit:	0.0
Fat (gm):	0	Bread:	0.0
Sat. fat (gm):	0	Meat:	0.0
Cholesterol (mg):	0	Fat:	0.0
Sodium (mg):	8		
Protein (gm):	0.2		
Carbohydrate (gm):	2.4		

TOMATO CHUTNEY

Good enough to eat by the spoonful! Drizzle over turkey burgers, cutlets, or grilled cheese sandwiches, for just a start.

Makes 4 cups

2 cups unpeeled, chopped tomatoes

2 cups unpeeled, chopped tart apples

³/₄ cup chopped onion

¹/₄ cup dark raisins

¹/₄ cup brown sugar, packed, *or* 3 tablespoons frozen apple juice concentrate

¹/₂ teaspoon powdered ginger

¹/₈ teaspoon allspice

¹/₈ teaspoon cayenne pepper

²/₃ cup cider vinegar

1. Combine all ingredients in a stainless steel or enameled saucepan. Heat to boiling. Reduce heat and simmer, uncovered, until thick, 45 to 55 minutes, stirring occasionally.

Microwave Method: Combine all ingredients in large microwave-safe bowl. Cook (high) 20 minutes, stirring every 5 minutes. Refrigerate.

Nutritional Data

PER ¹/₄-CUP SERVING		EXCHANGES	
Calories:	33	Milk:	0.0
% Calories from fat:	5	Vegetable:	0.1
Fat (gm):	0	Fruit:	0.4
Sat. fat (gm):	0	Bread:	0.1
Cholesterol (mg):	0	Meat:	0.0
Sodium (mg):	8	Fat:	0.0
Protein (gm):	0.2		
Carbohydrate (gm):	8.4		

SUN-DRIED TOMATOES

Sun-dried tomatoes are so highly concentrated that it takes 17 pounds of fresh tomatoes to make 1 pound of dried! Snip them with scissors and add to sandwich fillings, or dampen them and place whole on sandwiches.

Makes 1 quart*

16 medium tomatoes (Roma, Borghese cherry, or standard)

3 tablespoons (total) any combination of fresh rosemary, basil, or thyme leaves, optional

1. Wash and stem tomatoes. Slice horizontally, about 1/4-in. thick. Season with herbs or leave plain.

2. Lay on mesh or foil-covered baking sheets. Cover tomatoes lightly with cheesecloth. Choose drying method below: Sun, Oven, or Microwave.

Sun Method: Place in hot sun for several hours, turning occasionally, until dryness is achieved.

Oven Method: Bake in 200-degree oven about 7 hours. Watch carefully to make sure tomatoes do not burn.

Microwave Method: Place tomatoes cut side up on microwave baking sheet and bake (low) 14 to 18 minutes.

3. Store dry in jars in a cool pantry. Or marinate tomatoes by placing in jars with olive oil, garlic, and herbs. (Olive oil will cloud over, but the flavor will not be affected.) Refrigerate marinated tomatoes immediately at 40 degrees F. or below.

Note: It takes 8 medium size tomatoes to make 1 pint of sun-dried tomatoes.

Nutritional Data

PER 1/4-CUP SERVING		EXCHANGES	
Calories:	35	Milk:	0.0
% Calories from fat:	9	Vegetable:	0.0
Fat (gm):	0.4	Fruit:	0.0
Sat. fat (gm):	0.1	Bread:	0.5
Cholesterol (mg):	0	Meat:	0.1
Sodium (mg):	283	Fat:	0.1
Protein (gm):	1.9		
Carbohydrate (gm):	7.5		

ROASTED CHILI SALSA

While the barbecue grill is hot, throw on a few Anaheim chilies and an extra corn on the cob to make this salsa. Delicious over roast beef, turkey, or chicken sandwiches.

Makes 2 cups

- 1 large ear corn, roasted
- 6 Anaheim chilies, roasted, peeled, seeded, and chopped, *or* 2, 4-oz. cans roasted, peeled, and chopped chilies
- 1 large tomato, chopped
- 3/4 cup finely chopped jicama
- 1/3 cup minced onion
- 1/2 cup minced fresh cilantro
- 2 tablespoons lime juice
- 2 teaspoons sugar
- 1 clove garlic, crushed
- Salt and pepper, to taste

1. Combine all ingredients. Cover and chill.

Note: When working with fresh chilies, use rubber gloves and do not touch your face, particularly your eyes.

Nutritional Data

PER 1/4-CUP SERVING		EXCHANGES	
Calories:	32	Milk:	0.0
% Calories from fat:	5	Vegetable:	0.5
Fat (gm):	0	Fruit:	0.0
Sat. fat (gm):	0	Bread:	0.2
Cholesterol (mg):	0	Meat:	0.0
Sodium (mg):	69	Fat:	0.0
Protein (gm):	0.9		
Carbohydrate (gm):	7.1		

Salsa Fresca

Makes 2³/₄ cups

4 ripe tomatoes, cored, seeded, and finely
  chopped
¹/₃ cup lemon juice
¹/₄ cup chopped cilantro leaves
2 green onions, chopped, including greens
2 Anaheim chilies, seeded and finely chopped,
  or ¹/₂ cup canned diced green chilies
¹/₂ jalapeño chili, finely chopped

1. Combine all ingredients and refrigerate.

Note: When working with fresh chilies, use rubber gloves and do not touch
your face, particularly your eyes.

Nutritional Data

PER ¹/₄-CUP SERVING		EXCHANGES	
Calories:	18	Milk:	0.0
% Calories from fat:	7	Vegetable:	0.4
Fat (gm):	0	Fruit:	0.1
Sat. fat (gm):	0	Bread:	0.0
Cholesterol (mg):	0	Meat:	0.0
Sodium (mg):	11	Fat:	0.0
Protein (gm):	0.9		
Carbohydrate (gm):	3.8		

Natural Garlic Spread

Attention garlic lovers! This garlic spread can be made ahead and refrigerated for up to 3 days or frozen up to 3 months. And don't worry about garlic's "side-effects." Keep a supply of black licorice. It usually will counteract garlic breath. This spread is nice on vegetarian and cheese sandwiches.

Serves 4

3 bulbs garlic, cloves separated
1 teaspoon olive oil

1. Preheat oven to 325 degrees.

2. In a small, ovenproof pan, toss whole unpeeled garlic cloves with olive oil. Cover and bake 45 to 60 minutes or until garlic is tender. Press garlic through sieve or garlic press to remove skins.

3. Spread on good-quality toasted bread, buttered or plain, with whipped cream cheese or low-fat sour cream.

Nutritional Data

PER SERVING		EXCHANGES	
Calories:	14	Milk:	0.0
% Calories from fat:	20	Vegetable:	0.0
Fat (gm):	0	Fruit:	0.0
Sat. fat (gm):	0	Bread:	0.0
Cholesterol (mg):	0	Meat:	0.0
Sodium (mg):	0.7	Fat:	0.1
Protein (gm):	0.3		
Carbohydrate (gm):	2.4		

LEMON CREAM SPREAD

This cherry yellow spread brightens bagels and toast with just enough sweetness.

Makes 1¼ cups

- 1   10½-oz. pkg. extra-firm tofu
- 1   heaping tablespoon grated lemon rind
- 3   tablespoons lemon juice
- 4   tablespoons frozen apple juice concentrate, thawed
- 2–3   drops yellow food coloring
  Pinch of salt

1. Combine all ingredients except tofu in blender. Process, gradually dropping cubes or spoonfuls of tofu into blender container. Chill before serving.

Nutritional Data

PER 1-TABLESPOON SERVING		EXCHANGES	
Calories:	15	Milk:	0.0
% Calories from fat:	12	Vegetable:	0.0
Fat (gm):	0	Fruit:	0.2
Sat. fat (gm):	0	Bread:	0.0
Cholesterol (mg):	0	Meat:	0.1
Sodium (mg):	17	Fat:	0.0
Protein (gm):	1.2		
Carbohydrate (gm):	2.3		

High-Protein Tofu Mayonnaise

Tofu imparts the rich taste and consistency of regular mayonnaise. Tofu lasts up to 3 weeks in the refrigerator.

Makes 3 cups

- ³/₄ cup of water
- 1 teaspoon plain gelatin
- 19 ozs. extra-light tofu
- 1 tablespoon Dijon-style mustard
- ¹/₄ cup seasoned rice vinegar, *or* ¹/₄ cup rice vinegar plus 2 teaspoons sugar (or 1 packet sugar substitute)

1. Pour water into a measuring cup; microwave (high) just until water boils.

2. Combine gelatin and water in blender to soften; process until blended. Add remaining ingredients, adjusting seasoning to your taste.

Nutritional Data

PER 1-TABLESPOON SERVING		EXCHANGES	
Calories:	6	Milk:	0.0
% Calories from fat:	20	Vegetable:	0.0
Fat (gm):	0	Fruit:	0.0
Sat. fat (gm):	0	Bread:	0.0
Cholesterol (mg):	0	Meat:	0.1
Sodium (mg):	37	Fat:	0.0
Protein (gm):	1.2		
Carbohydrate (gm):	2.4		

CITRUS TARTAR SAUCE

Makes ⅝ cup

¼ cup nonfat mayonnaise
¼ cup nonfat sour cream
1 tablespoon fresh orange juice
2 teaspoons Dijon-style mustard
1 teaspoon freshly grated lemon peel
2 teaspoons sweet pickle relish

1. In a medium bowl, mix all ingredients, stirring well to combine. Refrigerate until serving. Sauce can be made up to 1 day in advance to allow flavors to blend.

Nutritional Data

PER 1-TABLESPOON SERVING

		EXCHANGES	
Calories:	12	Milk:	0.0
% Calories from fat:	5	Vegetable:	0.0
Fat (gm):	0.1	Fruit:	0.0
Sat. fat (gm):	0	Bread:	0.2
Cholesterol (mg):	0	Meat:	0.0
Sodium (mg):	125	Fat:	0.0
Protein (gm):	0.3		
Carbohydrate (gm):	2.8		

CALIFORNIA RANCH DRESSING

Makes 1¾ cups

½ cup buttermilk
⅝ cup light beer
½ cup nonfat mayonnaise
¼ Parmesan cheese
½ teaspoon dried dill weed, optional

1. Mix all ingredients in a blender. Cover and refrigerate.

Nutritional Data

PER 1-TABLESPOON SERVING

		EXCHANGES	
Calories:	11	Milk:	0.0
% Calories from fat:	24	Vegetable:	0.0
Fat (gm):	0.3	Fruit:	0.0
Sat. fat (gm):	0	Bread:	0.1
Cholesterol (mg):	0	Meat:	0.1
Sodium (mg):	75	Fat:	0.0
Protein (gm):	0.5		
Carbohydrate (gm):	1.2		

INSTANT FRUIT TOPPING

*Wonderful smothering pancakes or French toast. Blueberries
are high in fiber—4.4 grams per cup.*

Makes 3 cups

1 15-oz. can peaches in juice
1 tablespoon cornstarch
1/2 cup water, divided
1 pt. fresh, *or* frozen, blueberries, divided
1/2 teaspoon cinnamon
1/4 teaspoon allspice

1. Drain peaches and reserve juice. In medium saucepan, stir cornstarch into 2 tablespoons of water until dissolved. Stir in reserved water and peach juice. Bring to a boil, stirring for 1 minute.

2. Stir in peaches, half the blueberries, and spices. Cook 1 minute more, until thickened. Remove from heat and stir in remainder of blueberries. Serve hot or cold.

Nutritional Data

PER 1/2-CUP SERVING		EXCHANGES	
Calories:	50	Milk:	0.0
% Calories from fat:	2	Vegetable:	0.0
Fat (gm):	0.1	Fruit:	0.7
Sat. fat (gm):	0	Bread:	0.1
Cholesterol (mg):	0	Meat:	0.0
Sodium (mg):	3	Fat:	0.0
Protein (gm):	0.7		
Carbohydrate (gm):	12.5		

INDEX

The abbreviation "s." is used for "sandwich."